RUNNING A LIMITED COMPANY

Fourth Edition

RUNNING A LIMITED COMPANY

Fourth Edition

David Impey, MA
Solicitor, Director, Jordans Ltd

Nicholas Montague, FCA
Principal, Versatis

JORDANS

2001

Published by
Jordan Publishing Ltd
21 St Thomas Street
Bristol BS1 6JS

© Jordan Publishing Limited 2001
Reprinted December 2002
Reprinted May 2003
Reprinted April 2004
Reprinted September 2004

British Library Cataloguing-in-Publication Data
A catalogue record for this book is available from the British Library.

ISBN 0 85308 729 6

Typeset by Jordan Publishing Limited
Printed and bound in Great Britain by Bell & Bain Ltd, Glasgow

Preface

Running a limited company can be a complicated business. A company is a legal entity and the law makes many demands on the company itself and those who run it. These legal requirements must be fulfilled if the company and its officers are to avoid getting into trouble. For example, the directors of a private limited company are responsible for filing the company's accounts at Companies House within, ordinarily, 10 months of the end of the company's financial year and for filing an annual return each year. Failure to do so makes the company liable to a civil penalty, and can also mean that the directors are personally liable to a fine and a criminal record. Such problems may be avoided if the director and secretary have the basic information they need to carry out their duties and run the company smoothly.

This book is intended to serve as a practical guide to the requirements faced by a director, secretary or shareholder of a private company limited by shares registered in England and Wales, Scotland or Northern Ireland and to help them to understand and carry out their roles. It aims to complement the professional advice which the company's officers will receive from their solicitors and accountants, though it is not intended as a substitute for such advice. Indeed, many of the matters covered should not be considered without professional advice.

What this book will do is enable the reader to gain a better understanding of the way in which his or her business affairs are organised in the form of a limited company. It explains how to carry out the simpler operations which the company and its officers have to perform by law, and gives an indication of what the company's advisers will do in more complex situations. It will enable the officer to approach an outside adviser, armed with the information the adviser will require, thereby enabling a more economical service to be provided to the company.

These principles apply equally whether considering the application of the laws of England and Wales, the laws of Scotland or the laws of Northern Ireland, to the company. Much of the law of each jurisdiction is identical, but there are areas in which the law in one or more of them is different. Sometimes the different law applies only to companies registered in that jurisdiction. Sometimes it applies to all companies, wherever registered, which carry out a transaction governed by the law of that jurisdiction. The text makes clear the differences between rules in each jurisdiction and the extent to which the differences affect not only companies registered in that jurisdiction, but also other companies.

A unique feature of this book is its star-rating system which indicates the degree of need to take professional advice. One star means advice is desirable; two stars means it is strongly recommended; and three stars means it is crucial. Where a topic is given a no-star rating, it may usually be undertaken without professional advice – but remember, when in doubt, ask an expert. In this context, the importance of taking advice from a Scottish qualified professional in relation to Scottish matters and from a Northern Irish professional in relation to Northern Irish matters cannot be overstated.

Many people only seek the help of experts in times of difficulty. In terms of a company's future survival, that may already be too late. The key is in knowing when advice is needed and when it is not. Chapter 13 looks at the company's need to use lawyers, accountants and bankers. It analyses the do-it-yourself versus buy-it-in decision, sets out the surprisingly wide range of services on offer, and suggests how to get the most out of using professionals.

An informed director or secretary is not only better equipped to perform his or her duties with confidence in the normal course of events, but also has a better grasp of the more technical problems which are beyond the scope of his or her experience. He or she is more likely to know when and how to act and when not to act alone. The company can make more efficient use of professional advice – and an informed client is always a boon to the adviser.

Inevitably, there are a number of proposals as to law reform which are under consideration as this book goes to publication. Where these are relevant, they are referred to in the text. However, proposals are often modified and sometimes dropped altogether so that, when considering these reforms, professional advice will always be needed as to the current 'state of play'.

Certain terms used in the text include, unless the contrary is stated in the text, their Northern Ireland equivalents. For example, terms such as 'Act', 'section', 'Department of Trade and Industry' and 'Companies House' are deemed to include Northern Irish 'Orders', 'Articles', the 'Department of Economic Development' and the 'Northern Irish Companies Registry'.

Generally, where references are made to decisions of the Secretary of State for Trade and Industry (or, in Northern Ireland, the Department of Economic Development), these are in fact decisions taken on his behalf by the relevant Registrar of Companies unless the contrary is stated in the text. Throughout the rest of this book the personal pronoun 'he' is used. Its use is intended to encompass references to both males and females.

The law is stated as at 1 August 2001.

David Impey
Nicholas Montague
November 2001

Contents

CHAPTER 1

What is a Company?

The fundamental principle

There is one fundamental principle of company law from which all the rules and laws governing companies are derived. The company is recognised by the law as being a person. In legal jargon, a company has a separate and independent legal personality, distinct from its shareholders and directors.

'Persons' and 'individuals'

It follows that every time the word 'person' appears in an Act of Parliament, or is used by a lawyer or accountant, it includes not only a natural person, but also a company. The word 'individual', on the other hand, would refer only to a natural person. The strict legal meanings of these words will be used throughout this book.

Whilst an individual and a company are both recognised by the law as a person, a company is subject to many rules and limitations which either do not apply to an individual, or are different versions of the rules and limitations which apply to individuals. This book aims to help in understanding the reason for these rules and limitations.

'Business' and 'company'

A distinction must be drawn between the words 'business' and 'company'. A business is simply an activity. The activity should be thought of as quite distinct from the person or persons who carry it on – the two are separate. The person or persons carrying on the business may be either an individual, several individuals, or a company.

However, confusion is often caused by use of the word 'company' to refer to a business. This is inaccurate.

To confuse the meaning of 'business' and 'company' can be an expensive mistake. For example, an individual who wants to sell his *business* may put an advertisement in the newspaper which says '*company for sale*'. This is inaccurate, and will not impress a potential purchaser.

Similarly, a person who buys a defective item from a business owned by an individual, but who instructs his solicitor to sue 'the company' which sold it to him will confuse his solicitor – this is bound to make the exercise more expensive!

Business names

The situation is made more complicated by the fact that an individual, or a company, may carry on a business, and give it a name which is different from his or its own. This is called a 'business' or 'trading' name. It is quite lawful for a business name to include the words 'company' or '& company', even if the business is not carried on by a company. To avoid this confusion, and really find out who carries on a business, look at documents such as business letters received from the person carrying on the business. The name of the person or persons who are carrying on the business, and certain other details, must appear (unless there are more than 20 people carrying it on, in which case the business letters must state an address at which a list of the names of those persons is available for inspection). If the person carrying on the business is a company, the name of the company will therefore appear. It is easy to recognise a company name because it will end in 'Limited', 'Ltd', 'public limited company' or 'plc'. It is an offence for any other person other than a company to use a name which ends in any of these words or initials.

The name of the person carrying on the business may be in far smaller print than the business name which appears on such documents, but it must appear somewhere, and it must be legible. Business letters for customers, suppliers, etc, should always be checked. Do the letters make it clear who is carrying on the particular business? Is it an individual, or individuals, or a company? See Chapter 15 in respect of disclosure both on stationery and at premises.

In this book, the word 'name', when applied to a company, means its true corporate name, and not any business name which it might use.

A final word of warning. It is increasingly common to find oneself doing business with foreign entities. Some of these entities share many characteristics with our own limited companies – even to the extent that they may include, for example, 'Limited' or 'Ltd' in their names. However, any similarities should not disguise the fact that these are *not* UK companies, and due caution should be exercised in dealings with them.

Again, Chapter 15 will help recognise whether a company is in fact a UK company or is a foreign entity.

Starting up as a sole trader or in partnership

Most businesses start off by being carried on by individuals. An individual who carries on a business alone is called a 'sole trader'. Where two or more persons carry on a business together they are called 'partners' and their relationship is called a 'partnership'. Under English and Northern Irish law, it is very important to realise that a partnership is *not* itself a person, as a company is. The word 'partnership' is just a description of the relationship between two or more persons.

There are two special circumstances in which the word 'partnership' is used but the body referred to does have a legal personality of its own – it is a legal person distinct from the partners of whom it is composed.

First, in Scotland a partnership has always been recognised as a legal person in its own right. This does not mean that a Scottish partnership is really a company. It is still a partnership and shares the vast majority of its characteristics with an English partnership – it is just that Scottish partnership law is slightly different in this respect.

The same is not true of Limited Liability Partnerships. These are a new form of legal entity introduced throughout the UK on 6 April 2001. Despite the inclusion of the word 'Partnership' in the name of this new entity, it is in fact a legal person distinct from its members. This book does not deal with Limited Liability Partnerships. Where the term partnership is used, it refers to an ordinary partnership. Readers interested in learning more about Limited Liability Partnerships should refer to Whittaker, Machell and Ives *Limited Liability Partnerships: The New Law* (Jordans, 2001).

Forming a company and transferring the business

After a while, if the business grows, the sole trader or partners who carry on the business may form a company, and become its shareholders and directors. The business will then be sold to the company by the sole trader or partners – this is quite possible because the company is a separate legal person from the sole trader or partners, even if they are its directors and shareholders. In return for selling the business to the company, the sole trader or partners will receive shares in the company. This will constitute all, or a part of, their payment. In the case of partners who sell their business to a company, they will usually take a proportion of shares in the company which corresponds to the proportion of profits of the partnership to which they were entitled – what their lawyer would call their 'profit-sharing ratio'. For example:

Figure 1 – Sale of business to company which pays by issuing shares

Before the transaction, the business is carried on by the partners. Afterwards, it is carried on by the company. It appears that the partners have relinquished control of the business to the company and have lost the right to income from it; it is no longer their business. However, the shares in the company are owned by the partners, and the shares will usually confer rights which enable the shareholders to control the company and derive an income from it. For example, the shareholders have the right to vote on important matters relating to the company's affairs and to tell it and its directors what to do. They have the right to a dividend from the company if the business generates profits for the company. They also have the ultimate right to appoint and remove its directors – the people who manage the business of the company for them.

Alternatively, a company may be formed in order to start a business from scratch, rather than to buy an existing business. In that case, the shareholders will usually put cash into the company in payment for its shares. This provides the company with the means to start up and carry on the new business.

Acquisitions ***

Another common transaction is for an existing company to acquire control of an existing business from an individual, partnership or company with which it has no previous association or links, either as its only business, or in addition to its existing business(es).

There are a number of commercial and tax considerations as to the form and structure which such an acquisition should take in the particular circumstances. These mean that professional advice is always required.

Why a company? The two main reasons

Forming a company and complying with the requirements of the Companies Acts is a burden. Companies must be registered, and are subject to continuing disclosure requirements. One of the most significant burdens on a company is the need for its directors to prepare annual accounts. The accounts are filed with the registrar of companies and are therefore available for inspection by the public. Sole traders and partners do not have to suffer these burdens. So why should a company be formed at all?

The answer lies in the benefits which arise from the separate legal personality of the company in certain circumstances. The two main benefits which can arise from the company's legal personality are tax benefits and the benefits of limited liability. There are others, which will be looked at later.

Tax

The tax benefits can arise from the fact that the company is subject to its own special tax rules. If a business is carried on by a sole trader, he pays income tax on any profits, and capital gains tax on capital gains. The rule is exactly the same in partnership in that the partners' profits and gains are charged to income and capital gains tax in separate assessments. However, a company which carries on business pays only one tax, on both profits and gains. This tax is called 'corporation tax'.

The rates of income and capital gains tax and the rates of corporation tax are different. Not only are the rates different, but the profits and gains which are subject to tax are also worked out differently. The taxes are also assessed and payable at different times.

The amount of profit which directors and shareholders wish to distribute from the company is also relevant when comparing the tax bill in the two different circumstances. Profits and gains which are taxed to corporation tax going into the company will also be taxed to income tax coming out of it, and into the pockets of its directors and shareholders, so the comparison between the two circumstances is more complicated than it first appears.

However, the general result of the differences between the two tax regimes is that the more profitable a business becomes, the more likely it is that corporation tax rules will produce a lower overall tax bill than the income and capital gains tax rules.

This is why a business often begins by being owned by a sole trader or partners but, when it grows larger, is transferred by them to a company formed for that purpose.

At what stage should a sole trader, or partners, form a company and sell their business to it in return for a shareholding in the new company?

Unfortunately, there is no overall magic figure at which a sole trader or partner automatically knows that a company should be formed – each case will depend upon many circumstances, and will require a complicated calculation.

Particular sole traders or partners will need professional advice as to the appropriate time to form their own company. However, the bigger the profits, and the more sharply they are rising, the more likely it is that a company will be appropriate. Involving the professional adviser in the business on a regular basis is crucial to ensure that the company is formed at the right time.

Limited liability of a company's shareholders

The second main benefit flowing from the company's separate legal personality is that of limited liability.

Limited liability means that, in the case of a company whose business is not doing well, the shareholders of the company do not have to help the company pay its debts and discharge its liabilities. The business does not belong to them, it belongs to the company. It is the company which has the debts and liabilities, not its shareholders. The company and its shareholders are separate legal persons. The shareholders do, of course, have to pay the company any money owing on their shares. However, if the shares are fully paid for (and, in the case of a private company, they invariably are), no further money is payable by the shareholders under company law. In these circumstances, the *liability* of each shareholder for the debts of the company is said to be *limited* to the amount outstanding (if any) on his shares. In legal jargon, the shareholders have limited liability.

It is interesting that the common expression a 'company with limited liability' is not strictly accurate. It is not the company which has limited liability, it is its shareholders. The company's liability for the debts of its business is unlimited, and it may end up insolvent (unable to pay its debts) if the debts of its business are sufficiently large.

Of course, a sole trader, or partners, carrying on business are in the same position as the company. They carry on the business themselves, and must pay the debts of the business if things go wrong – their liability is unlimited, and they may end up insolvent.

Indeed, if a business is carried on by partners, their liability for the debts of the business carried on by them is said to be 'joint and several' under English and Northern Irish law. This means that one partner can be sued for the whole amount owed by all the partners; for example, if the others cannot afford to pay or have disappeared. It is not enough for the one partner to simply pay his proportion of the debt. So one partner may have to pay all the partnership debts either because he is richer than the others, or simply because he is available to be sued, and they are not. Of course, in those circumstances, he is entitled to sue his partners for reimbursement, but if they have no money, or have disappeared, this remedy will be useless.

The laws of England and Wales and Northern Ireland differ from those of Scotland in this respect. Since a Scottish partnership *is* a legal person, the partners cannot be sued directly for a liability of the partnership. However, once liability has been established against the partnership, the individual partners may still be liable, jointly and severally, without limit, for the debts and liabilities of the partnership in those proceedings. Ultimately, therefore, in common with partnerships in England and Wales and Northern Ireland, the liability of partners will be unlimited in respect of any debts which the firm is unable to satisfy.

Limited liability for the shareholders is therefore a good reason why a large, risky or highly profitable business is more likely to be carried on by a company. If the business carried on by the company goes wrong, it is the company which will be taken to court, and not its shareholders, whereas, if the business of a sole trader or partnership goes wrong, it is the sole trader or partners who will be taken to court.

Personal guarantees

Of course, the shareholders or directors of a company may have to help the company pay its debts if they have expressly agreed to. A bank, for example, may demand a personal guarantee from a shareholder or director if his company borrows money, saying that if the company defaults in repaying a loan, the shareholder or director will repay it. The shareholder or director may be asked to give a mortgage over his home as well.

Unfortunately for the individuals concerned, this is extremely common in the case of small or start-up businesses. The extent of the personal guarantee or mortgage required to be given is often such that the benefit of limited liability is negated for such individuals. However, these obligations are personal, and do not arise from company law.

Director's liability

The directors of a company may also be asked to help the company pay its debts, but only if they have acted fraudulently or in a way defined as improper by company legislation. However, a director who takes regular professional advice should never have to contribute towards the company's debts (see Chapter 12).

Publication of its affairs

It is because the shareholders of a company have limited liability that the company is obliged to make certain of its affairs public. A person who is dealing with a company knows he cannot sue the shareholders, but he can sue the company; so he needs to know about the company. Details of the company's affairs are usually made public by completion of special forms, or by setting information out on documents which are prepared in a particular format, so they are easy to find and understand on the company's public record. The company makes its affairs public both by lodging these special forms and documents with the relevant Registrar of Companies, and by keeping certain of its internal records open to inspection by members of the public. For a person to know that these forms, documents and records are publicly available, he needs to know that he is dealing with a company. As we have seen earlier in this chapter, the name of a private company must include 'Limited' or 'Ltd' and, in the case of a public company, 'public limited company' or 'plc' and the appearance of these words will alert him to this. The person dealing with the company can then make further enquiries, if he wishes, of the Registrar of Companies, or may inspect such of the company's internal records as are available for inspection.

Other advantages of forming a company

There are other advantages which flow from the company's separate legal personality.

Separation of control and management

A shareholder can control a company which is carrying on a business, and receive a dividend if the company's business makes a profit, without having to become involved in the day-to-day running of the business. The same is not usually true of a sole trader or partners. For example, partners carrying on a business know that they will have to pay the debts of the business if it goes wrong, so they will be reluctant to entrust the management of the business to someone else. Even if the size of the business requires the appointment of managers, the partners will probably take an active interest on a day-to-day basis.

Shareholders, on the other hand, have the protection of limited liability. They are therefore more likely to allow their company's business to be managed by someone else without intervening on a day-to-day basis. Company law therefore provides that the shareholders have power to appoint (and remove) special managers, who are called directors, to manage the business of the company. The directors are given stewardship, or custody, of the business of the company.

Since the directors are in a position of trust – looking after the company's business for it – they are subject to all sorts of duties and liabilities. These duties and liabilities are onerous, so that the shareholders and their company are given protection against abuse of their position by the directors.

Of course, a shareholder may also be a director, and often the shareholders and directors are the same people. However, company law deals with directors and shareholders separately. The directors must still observe all of these duties and liabilities when acting as directors, even if they are also the shareholders.

New participants

A consequent advantage of this separation of control of the company (shareholders) and management of its business (directors) is that the introduction of a new shareholder into the company is usually easier than introduction of a new partner into a partnership.

A new partner is jointly and severally liable for the debts of the business of the partnership, just as much as the most senior or longest-established partner. The new partner will therefore argue that he should have an equal, or substantial, say in how the business is run, and an adequate share in the profits, to recompense him for his risk. The existing partners may disagree. There is much scope for negotiation. A new shareholder in a company, on the other hand, knows that if the company's business is run well, he may receive dividends and the value of his shares in the company should rise, but if the business runs into difficulties, he has limited liability. Consequently, all a new shareholder may be concerned about is whether the business carried on by a company is likely to be profitable, and whether the directors are competent. He will not necessarily be interested in participating in day-to-day management.

Raising capital

Of course, this means that it is often easier for a company to raise new money than it is for a partnership. A person will be far more cautious about putting his money into a partnership by becoming a partner (since he will have joint and several unlimited liability), than he will be about putting his money into a company by buying shares (since he will have the protection of limited liability).

Employees and family members

For example, members of a shareholder's family, such as children, may buy shares in the company, or have them bought for them, or given to them. In the case of children under 18 the shares will usually be held on their behalf by trustees under a family trust. If the company is profitable, they (or the trustees on their behalf) may receive dividends. If not, they have limited liability. Limited liability also means that, by gradually increasing the number of shares held by his family a majority shareholder can shift control of the company to his family – leaving it in their hands on his retirement. Introducing family members into a partnership and providing for succession to the partnership business is far more complex.

Employees may also be encouraged to work harder if they and their families are given the opportunity to buy shares in their company. Sole traders and partners are not able to offer incentives to their employees so simply.

The tax laws encourage members of families and employees to buy shares by providing tax incentives if the shares are held in particular ways. For family members there can be advantages in putting shares into special trusts to benefit children. For employees, certain types of share scheme allow employees and their families to buy shares, or the right to buy shares (share options), in their companies, and obtain tax reliefs. Such schemes may be for certain higher-paid employees, or all employees, depending on the sort of scheme the company wishes to operate.

Outside investors

Complete outsiders are also encouraged by the tax laws to approach companies and ask to buy their shares. Under the Enterprise Investment Scheme, a person may invest in certain companies by buying their shares and, if certain conditions are met, will obtain tax relief on his investment. Some of the conditions relate to the business carried on by the company (which must be a 'qualifying trade'), the amount invested, and the length of time the shares are held. A Venture Capital Trust also exists, the aim of which is to encourage investment in unquoted companies by offering tax incentives to attract investors in smaller private companies.

Groups of companies

Another benefit of a company's legal personality is the ability to create a group of companies. There are different rules for determining whether a group of companies exists for accounting purposes (ie in deciding whether 'group accounts' must be prepared) as against determining whether there is a group for general company law purposes. Under the general company law rules, the most common way of creating a group is by ensuring that a majority of the voting shares of a company or companies are owned by another company or companies. At the top of the resulting 'family tree' will be the 'holding' or 'parent' company. Such companies are entitled to include the word 'holdings' or 'group' in their name, although this is not obligatory. All the others will be 'subsidiary' companies. Examples of groups are:

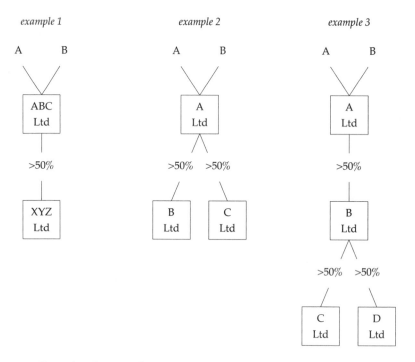

Figure 2 – Examples of groups of companies

It can be seen that one parent company may have many subsidiaries. Similarly, one subsidiary may have more than one parent company. In the third example above, C Ltd and D Ltd both have two parent companies. B Ltd is the *immediate* parent company, and A Ltd is the *ultimate* parent company of both.

   If the ultimate parent company is a public company whose shares are 'quoted' or 'listed' on the Stock Exchange or the Alternative Investment Market, the value of those shares will appear in the financial press and the shareholder can tell from the value of his shares in the parent company how the group as a whole is doing.

More often, the ultimate parent company is a private company, so that the value of the shares will not be publicly quoted. The value of such shares is often difficult to determine, and will frequently be the subject of negotiation each time a value is needed, such as on a sale of shares, or death of a shareholder.

However, in the absence of any other means whereby A Ltd controls B Ltd (or vice versa), there is *not* a group in the following circumstances:

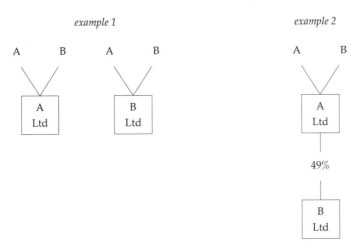

Figure 3 – Examples of non-groups of companies

The advantage of a group of companies is that each subsidiary can carry on a different business. If one business fails, the company carrying it on may become insolvent, but the other companies in the group will not. However, if the businesses are successful, the use of subsidiaries provides a clear means of keeping the results of each business separate, to assess its profitability or productivity. The parent company may also carry on its own business (or provide central and/or management services), but often it acts simply as a central fund, collecting dividends from its subsidiaries, which it can then use to pay dividends to its own shareholders.

Tax laws provide advantages and reliefs to groups of companies. The reliefs vary, usually according to the proportion of shares in a subsidiary which is held by its immediate parent company. To obtain maximum tax benefits, most groups will comprise one ultimate parent company and one or more wholly owned subsidiaries. A subsidiary is 'wholly owned' if all its shares are controlled by another company – it is not necessary for every share to be owned outright by the parent. However, it is not always commercially possible or desirable for a subsidiary to be wholly owned. For example, the subsidiary may have been set up as a joint-venture company, with another organisation holding some of its shares. Alternatively, the long or medium-term intention of the group may be to build a business up and sell it off. 'Parcelling' the business into a separate limited company, and selling the shares in the subsidiary company, either wholly, or in instalments, may be a much more efficient way of doing this than selling the business itself.

Every few years, a group of companies may be reorganised, with the intention of creating a more efficient structure for the group to trade as a whole. Such reorganisations are often complex, and should not be carried out without professional advice. There are always commercial *and* tax implications to be considered.

Companies within a group will often trade with one another – one providing products or services which complement those of another. For example, one may provide raw materials for a manufacturing process of another.

Of course, there are also disadvantages in forming a group of companies. It is not always wise to have a group of companies instead of one single company for the following reasons.

Taxation

Corporation tax is charged at three rates: the 'starting rate', a low rate on a first band of income, the 'small companies' rate and the full rate. If a company has no connections with any other companies (it is not in a group or associated with another company in any way), then the rate at which tax is charged depends on the company's taxable profits. For example, if profits are lower than a certain figure, which is reviewed in the budget every year, the small companies rate will apply.

If the company's profits figure is above the figure for small companies, but below the figure for the standard rate, there are marginal rates for the excess profit over the figure for small companies.

If, on the other hand, there are two related companies, one generating less than the profits figure for small companies and the other generating sufficient profits to be taxed at a marginal rate, the rules become complex because of the relationship between the two companies. Tax planning with groups needs professional advice and great care.

Administration

As mentioned already, each company must prepare annual accounts and submit them to the registrar of companies. The accounts of most companies must be audited (certified as presenting a true and fair view of the company's affairs) by a 'registered auditor'. However, smaller companies are usually exempt from the audit requirement. These rules are dealt with in more detail in Chapter 9. Various other requirements have to be observed each year. Each company will require a separate book-keeping system and the administration generally will be more complicated than having a single company.

It is necessary to take professional advice to determine the benefits and burdens of having more than one company, and make the decision accordingly.

The intention here has been to describe only very generally the concept and principles of groups of companies. Setting up a group is an area where professional advice should be taken at every stage as there are many pitfalls to trap the unwary, especially on the taxation side, which can become very complex.

Status

Another advantage of forming a company relates solely to status. Even though there are many large and reputable businesses carried on by sole traders or partners, the public assume, sometimes wrongly, that a company is more likely to continue in business, and pay its debts, and that a company will be more reputable, than a sole trader or partners.

Often this is true. The benefits of tax and limited liability mean that a company's business is usually of a certain size. It also means that the company is subject to all the formalities and publicity requirements which attach to companies, and this may be indicative of its standing, since such requirements are a disincentive to the frivolous.

Borrowing

For these reasons, banks are often, as a very general rule, more prepared to lend money to companies than sole traders or partners. The bank will also know that a company can create a special sort of mortgage or charge over its property – a floating charge – as a security for money it borrows, which a sole trader, or partners, cannot. (However, do not expect the bank to dispense automatically with the need for personal guarantees from the company's shareholders and directors if a substantial sum is borrowed by their company, even if the company can give a mortgage over its property as security.)

Private and public companies

It is appropriate at this point to define the difference between a private and a public company. Both private and public companies give their shareholders the protection of limited liability – it is not accurate to refer, as many do, to a company which re-registers from private to public as going from limited to public. However, the vast majority of companies are private. So how can one tell if a company is private or public? The Companies Acts say that a company is public if its memorandum of association says that it is. All other companies are private. The Acts then go on to specify a number of benefits and burdens which apply only to public companies.

Company name

The most obvious difference is that the name of a public company must end in 'public limited company' or 'plc'. It is a criminal offence for any other company or business name to end in these words or initials.

Offers to the public

Another important difference is that a public company is allowed to offer its shares to the public, but a private company cannot. This means that a public company can send out circulars and advertise in newspapers, etc, offering to sell, or inviting people to buy, its shares, but a private company cannot. The only people to whom a *private* company can normally offer its shares are its existing shareholders and employees and their families, and any debenture-holders (see Chapter 10).

Of course, a person who approaches a private company may buy its shares, but the private company may not itself offer its shares to that person or invite him to apply for them – it cannot take the initiative.

Since the public may find themselves being offered shares by a public company, company law provides them with certain protections. For example, rules made by, and pursuant to, the Companies and Financial Services Acts require that a public company which offers its shares to the public must give the public certain information about itself, in writing, when making such an offer. Whether the offer is made in a circular, advertisement or any other way (including by electronic means), the company must publish this information in a 'prospectus' or 'listing particulars' and make the prospectus or particulars available to the public free of charge.

Share capital

The Companies Acts also state that a public company must have an issued share capital of at least £50,000 with each share paid up by at least one-quarter. For example, if the company has shares of £1, 25p must have been paid by the shareholders, on each issued share. Additionally, if the shareholders have agreed to pay the company more than £1 for those shares (they have agreed to pay 'a premium'), the premium must also be paid. Until such requirements have been satisfied, a public company may not trade or borrow money. As proof of satisfaction of these requirements, a public company must have been issued with a trading certificate by the Registrar of Companies. This contrasts with a private company, which may trade or borrow money immediately it is incorporated, even if it has only one shareholder, holding only one share.

Directors

A public company must have at least two directors, who must retire at 70 unless certain procedural requirements are met, and its secretary must fall within certain categories set out in the Companies Acts. These categories –

chartered secretary, accountant, solicitor, etc, – are intended to ensure that the secretary of a public company has a certain competence and familiarity with company matters. A private company may have only one director, if its articles allow, and, unless the company is a subsidiary of a public company, a director may be of any age. The secretary of a private company need meet no particular criteria.

Technical limitations

There are various other technical limitations on public companies in the Companies Acts – for example, they may not declare dividends as freely as private companies and there are stricter rules regarding the contents of their audited accounts.

Listed companies

However, none of these limitations confers absolute protection on the public, so that a public company may find it difficult to attract new shareholders when offering shares to the public. How can it make its shares more attractive?

The answer lies in the company applying for its shares to be admitted to a 'listing' or 'quotation', so that they are bought and sold in a particular 'market'. If the company's shares are 'listed' or 'quoted', the public knows that the company has met additional requirements, far and above those set for public companies by the Companies Acts, and will therefore be more inclined to buy the shares of that company if offered to them. In effect, by meeting these requirements, the company is demonstrating that it has good credentials and standing.

There are two main markets in the UK. If a company's shares are to be listed or quoted on either market, it must comply with the admission requirements for that market. The junior market is the Alternative Investment Market (known as 'AIM'). The senior market is the Official List of the London Stock Exchange. It is hard to get shares onto AIM, but even harder to get them onto the Official List of the London Stock Exchange. However, once a company's shares are dealt with on either of these markets, the public will buy them with greater confidence, because they know that the company will have had to satisfy their respective admission requirements. A company's shares will only be dealt with on one market at a time. Of course, not all public companies' shares are bought and sold on either of these markets. Most public companies' shares are not listed or quoted. Many potential investors make the assumption that, if it is public, it is listed. This is not the case.

Indeed, there are many public companies which do not even offer their shares to the public. The articles of such companies may operate much as a private company. Such companies are often public for the simple commercial reason that a customer may feel safer buying from a public company – the words 'public limited company' or letters 'plc' at the end of the name give added confidence. A significant number of companies re-register from private to public every year. The usual reason is to acquire a new kudos or status in their commercial activities, rather than to enable them to offer shares to the public. Still less, in order to apply for a listing on one of the two main markets.

Name protection

Another reason for forming a company is simply for name protection purposes. Of course, a person carrying on a business acquires a certain amount of protection for the name of the business (or the name of a particular product or a brand name), simply by using it. The use of a name in such a way that it is associated by the public with a particular business enables the person carrying on that business to take another person to court if the other has traded off his reputation by using the same or a similar business name. See Chapter 2 for such rights. Further protection can be obtained for a business name by registering the name on the companies index. If the business name is the same as the name of a company carrying on the business, the name is, of course, already registered. However, the business name may be different from the name of the company, or the name may be that of a business carried on by a sole trader or partnership, which is not required to be registered on the companies index. Consequently, to protect that name, companies are sometimes formed which will not carry on any business whatsoever. They will, however, have the same name as a particular business carried on or to be carried on by a sole trader or partnership, or even a company registered in a different name. The effect of forming a company in that name is to put the name on a public register in circumstances where it would not otherwise appear on any public register. Another person planning to use the name, or a similar name, and making the usual name checking searches and inquiries is therefore warned off when he sees that the name is registered as a company name. See Chapter 2 for such searches and inquiries.

Such a company will invariably be either a 'dormant' or an 'audit exempt' company. In consequence, all it need lodge at Companies House in each year are unaudited accounts, an annual return, and the annual return fee. No auditors' fees are incurred, although it may be necessary to pay an accountant to prepare the unaudited accounts. See Chapter 9 for a more detailed consideration of accounting matters.

Taxation

There can be other taxation considerations in forming a company, notably in relation to the provision of pensions, and of benefits such as cars. The company accountant plays a crucial role in advising on such matters.

Disadvantages

However, this chapter must end in stressing the disadvantages of running a company.

The formalities of forming the company, and the administrative burden of making its affairs public are obvious, but perhaps the greatest practical disadvantage lies in having continually to remember to draw the distinction between directors and shareholders, and the respective restraints and requirements on their behaviour. A person who is both a director and a shareholder, must always remember in what capacity he is acting at any given moment. The considerations he must have in mind as a director are very onerous, and very different from those he must have in mind as a shareholder.

Additionally, both the shareholders and the directors must remember that the business being carried on is not their business. It belongs to the company, and they must always be aware of this. A classic illustration of this is that ex-partners, who are now directors of a company, often find it difficult to accept that they may not make 'drawings', as they did when they were in partnership, from the company – companies are not able to make loans to directors except in very specific and limited circumstances.

CHAPTER 2

The Company and its Constitution

Forming the company

Whilst a natural person is born, artificial persons must be formed procedurally. A company is formed by following a procedure which is set out in the Companies Acts. The procedure requires filing of documents and a fee with a registrar of companies. There are three registrars in the UK – with registries in Cardiff, Edinburgh and Belfast. There are also branches of these main registries – for example, there is a branch of the Cardiff registry in London, at which documents may be filed, and searches made. For convenience the general term 'Companies House' has been used in this book wherever reference is made to any of the registries.

It is only when the registrar with whom documents are filed issues a certificate of incorporation that the company is in existence. Anyone who makes an agreement on behalf of a company before it is in existence will be personally liable on that agreement, even after the company comes into existence. Such agreements are called 'pre-formation' or 'pre-incorporation' contracts. Legal advice should always be taken before making a pre-incorporation contract. Pre-incorporation contracts need not be in writing, so the absence of a document does not necessarily mean there is no pre-incorporation contract.

When the certificate of incorporation is issued, the company is said to have been created, registered, formed or incorporated. The certificate will state name, date of incorporation and a unique company number. Whilst the name may be changed, the number will stay constant until the company is dissolved. There are no rules as to where the certificate should be kept. Many companies like to display the certificate at the registered office, or a place of business, but this is not a legal requirement. If it is not displayed, it is good practice to keep it with the company's registers, at the registered office.

If the certificate is lost, the registrar will issue a duplicate, upon payment of a fee. The duplicate may be used for all the same purposes as the original.

Ordinarily, the only time when the company will need to produce its certificate is to open a bank account, to deal with overseas authorities or lawyers, or to apply for tax clearance on certain complicated transactions.

Private companies may carry on business immediately upon issue of a certificate of incorporation. A public company must obtain a trading certificate. See Chapter 1 in this respect.

The memorandum of association **

Every company, whether private or public, must have a memorandum of association. If the company is private, this document must contain five clauses. These are discussed below. If the company is public, there must also be a statement that the company is to be a public company. The proposed shareholders of the company will decide the contents of the memorandum, although certain matters must be included. The shareholders of the company may change certain parts of the memorandum once the company has been formed, if this becomes necessary, or desirable.

The name

First, the memorandum must state the name of the company. The reader is reminded of the distinction between the company name and any business name to be used by the company. It is the company name which must appear in the memorandum.

There are a number of rules which apply to names, which must be observed both when the company is incorporated, and if it subsequently wishes to change its name.

'Limited' or 'Ltd'

The name of a private company must either end in the word 'Limited' or 'Ltd' so that the public know that they are dealing with a company. The shareholders of the company must make a choice as to which they want. Incorporation papers should not be submitted in which the name appears with one ending in one part, and the other ending in another part. The registrar requires consistency, because he has to be clear as to which version to include on the certificate of incorporation. Once incorporated, it is uncertain whether a company with a certificate of incorporation stating that the name end is 'Limited' can use 'Ltd' as an abbreviation – for example, on its stationery. The courts have not been consistent in their attitude to the use of 'Ltd' as an abbreviation of 'Limited', so it is prudent not to use it as such.

There are special rules for companies with a registered office in Wales, which may use Welsh equivalents of 'Limited' and 'Ltd'.

Refusal of registration

A name will be refused for registration if:

(1)   it is the same as a name already appearing on the list of company names at Companies House ('the companies index'); or
(2)   its use would constitute a criminal offence; or
(3)   it is offensive.

Both (2) and (3) are determined by the registrar of companies (for the Secretary of State for Trade and Industry) as matters of opinion.

'Sensitive' words

A name will also be refused registration if it contains a 'sensitive' word, unless the written consent of particular bodies have been obtained, or the use is justified by a written assurance from a proposed officer of the company (a director or the secretary), a solicitor, accountant, or company registration agent, that the company meets certain criteria. Current lists of sensitive words for each of Great Britain and Northern Ireland appear in Appendix B – although the lists are amended from time to time, and should be re-checked on each incorporation (or change of name). The rules on sensitive words can be checked on www.companieshouse.gov.uk. Words are usually sensitive if they imply a certain prestige or eminence. For example, if a company wishes to include the word 'international' in its name as a suffix, an assurance must be given that it will trade in at least two overseas countries.

Similar names

IS THE PROPOSED COMPANY NAME SIMILAR TO A NAME ALREADY ON THE COMPANIES INDEX? Care must be taken to ensure that the proposed name is not similar to a name already on the companies index. The registrars of companies for Scotland, and England and Wales, amalgamate the companies registered with them into one companies' index for the purpose of determining whether a name is the same as a name already registered. Thus a company may not be registered in Scotland with a name which has already been registered in England and Wales, and vice versa. The proposed name will not be refused registration by Companies House because it is similar to a name already on the index, but a new company may find that another company already on the companies index may:

(1)   object to the Secretary of State for Trade and Industry within 12 months of the new name appearing on the index, that the new name is 'too like' its own; or
(2)   bring a 'passing-off' action in the courts.

When considering whether names are 'too like', the Secretary of State and the courts apply different criteria. The Secretary of State will simply ask whether the names are in fact similar. His aim is to ensure that, for example, a person seeking to carry out a search against a company is not presented with two very similarly named companies and cannot easily work out which is which. He will ignore the fact they may be in different geographical locations or different trades or businesses.

In fact, the Secretary of State may take action against a company on the grounds that its name is 'too like' that of another company on his own initiative, even if he has not received an objection from another company.

Business people may therefore consider asking an experienced searcher to check the companies index for them to ensure their proposed name is not 'too like' that of an existing company. They should do this both on incorporation of a new company and on change of name of an existing company. Professional advisers or a company registration agent will offer such a service. Particularly, they will be aware of special rules – for example, the Secretary of State ignores symbols such as '@' or expressions such as '.com' or 'www' in company names when considering whether they are 'too like'. There are many such rules to take into account.

The courts will take a wider view and ask not only whether the names are in fact similar but also whether the public have been misled and confused. They will therefore take into account factors such as the nature of the business and the location of each.

Both may order a company to change its name, with all the attendant expense and inconvenience regarding new stationery, promotional costs, etc, and the courts may award damages against it.

IS THE PROPOSED COMPANY NAME SIMILAR TO A BUSINESS NAME ALREADY IN USE? Inquiries must also be made to ensure that the proposed company name is not similar to a business name already in use. Where the similarity is between a proposed company name and an existing business name, the Secretary of State will not be interested if an objection is made to him. He is only concerned with similar *company* names. However, a passing-off action is still possible. Once again, professional advice should be sought. The companies index will not reveal business names, so where can a search be made? There is no register of business names but a professional adviser might recommend and carry out a search in the trade and service marks register or other special registers. However, there should also be extensive checking in trade journals, *Yellow Pages*, etc, by the directors. Many business, product or brand names are registered as domain names on the internet or are mentioned in websites or by visitors to chatrooms. Particular names can be checked against registered domain names under top level domains such as .com, .net and .org and country code top level domains such as .uk, at www.whois.co.uk. Search engines such as www.google.com can be used to search the web generally. Of course, if the company is taking over the business name used previously by a sole trader or partnership, and merely adding 'Limited' there is less likely to be a problem.

In all searches and inquiries, the company is looking for names which are similar enough to the company's, so that the public are misled into confusing the two names. For example, Abkem Limited and Abchem Limited are obviously similar and confusing. There may be other less obviously similar names which also cause confusion.

IS THE PROPOSED BUSINESS NAME OF A COMPANY SIMILAR TO AN EXISTING NAME OR EXISTING BUSINESS NAME? If any company is going to use a business name it should carry out the same checks and inquiries as it did for its company name, to ensure that the business name is not similar to company names, and other business names, already in use. If it is, there is the danger of a passing-off action.

PROTECTING A COMPANY NAME OR A BUSINESS NAME. Other ways of protecting both the company name or any business name should also be considered when choosing either type of name. For example, registration of a name, logo or combination of the two, as a trade mark can confer substantial protection against its unauthorised use by another. However, if it is intended to register a name as a trade or service mark, the name must be capable of registration at the Trade Marks Registry in the UK. If the company is to trade outside the UK, it may consider registering a trade mark at other national registries. There are also registration systems that offer protection in a number of countries. For example, registration of a European Community trade mark at the European Community registry in Alicante offers protection in every EU country, without the need for individual registrations in national registries. This ordinarily requires that the name or business name be distinctive.

Clearly, choice of a name or a business name is a complicated matter. Legal advice should always be taken.

Changing a company name or a business name

A company may change its name by a special resolution of its shareholders. Business names, on the other hand, may be chosen and changed by the directors. The same checks should always be made on a change of name or business name as are made when choosing an initial name.

A special resolution to change the company's name must be filed with the registrar of companies. It is not until the registrar issues a certificate evidencing the change of name that the change of name is effective.

The company should take great care not to order new stationery, etc, in the new name until either the certificate is issued, or the company is quite sure that it will be.

Monitoring company and business names (see figures 4 and 5)

Once a company has registered and used its name, or started using a business name, it must ensure that it is aware of any new company names or business names which are registered or used, and which are similar to its own, so that it can take action to protect its name or business name.

It might make regular name checks through its advisers or search agents, or subscribe to a name-watching service, as well as using the grapevine. The companies index, trade mark registrations and the web can all be monitored.

Taking legal action ***

The bringing or defending of any objection or action can involve substantial expense. Professional advice will always be required, and it will be necessary to explore and co-ordinate all possible legal remedies. For example, the objection and/or action may also give rise to possible action for breach of other 'intellectual property rights' such as copyrights, designs or patents, and all remedies pursued should be co-ordinated if they are to be achieved.

Domicile

The second clause in the memorandum states where the registered office of the company is to be located. It should state either England and Wales, Scotland or Northern Ireland and not the actual address of the registered office. This determines which registrar of companies has jurisdiction over the company, and where it sends information about itself. For example, a company which states that its registered office is to be located in England and Wales is said to be domiciled there and will be subject to the rules of the registrar of companies in Cardiff. Once the domicile of a company has been chosen, it cannot be changed. For example, the registered office of a company registered in Scotland must be in Scotland. It cannot be changed to an address in, for example, England and Wales or Northern Ireland. Of course, there are no constraints on a company trading in other jurisdictions, irrespective of where it is registered. Finally, a company domiciled in, for example, England and Wales can move its registered office freely *within* England and Wales.

It is possible for the memorandum to state that the company's registered office is to be located only in Wales, rather than England and Wales. This permits the company to deliver some documents to the registrar of companies in Welsh.

This clause in the memorandum cannot be changed.

OWNER OF A BUSINESS NAME
(whether sole trader, partner or company)

To protect the name	Consider registering a dormant company so the name is made public	Consider registering a trade mark for name protection purposes	Consider registering domain names under both the generic top level domains (.com etc) and relevant country code top level domains (.uk, .fr etc)	Monitor or periodically check the companies index and trade marks register	Monitor or periodically check the internet for domain name registrations and the web for mention of the name	Monitor or periodically check *Yellow Pages*, trade journals, etc and 'the grapevine'
If there is a similar or identical name	Consider a passing-off action or an objection to the registrar of companies	Consider a passing-off action and action under trade mark law	Consider a passing-off action	Consider a passing-off action and, if registered as a company, an objection to the registrar of companies and, if registered as a trade mark, under trade mark law		

Figure 4 – Business name

COMPANY NAME

To protect the name

- Fact of registration on the companies index makes the name public
- Consider registering a trade mark for name protection purposes
- Consider registering domain names under both the generic top level domains (.com etc) and relevant country code top level domains (.uk, .fr etc)
- Monitor or periodically check the companies index and trade marks register
- Monitor or periodically check the internet for domain name registrations and the web for mention of the name
- Monitor or periodically check *Yellow Pages*, trade journals, etc and 'the grapevine'

If there is a similar or identical name

- Consider a passing-off action or an objection to the registrar of companies
- Consider a passing-off action and action under trade mark law
- Consider a passing-off action
- Consider a passing-off action, an objection to the registrar of companies and, if registered as a trade mark, under trade mark law

Figure 5 – Company name

The objects and powers

The Companies Acts require a company to state its objects – the activities for which it was incorporated. This statement of objects must appear in the memorandum. Whilst the company is recognised as a person in law, it must not carry on any activity which is not specified in this statement. It is the shareholders who decide upon the contents of the memorandum in this respect.

To ensure that companies can do everything an individual can do, shareholders have traditionally allowed their companies to have a very long statement of objects, divided into many paragraphs. These are called objects clauses. It has also been the practice to set out, in the same statement, all of the ancillary and subsidiary transactions which a company may need to carry out in order to achieve its objects. For example, the power for the company to borrow money, sell parts of its business, and buy new businesses. The clauses setting out these transactions are called the company's 'powers'. The maxim has always been 'if in doubt, put it in'. However, company legislation now contains provisions which mean that objects and powers of modern companies may be far shorter. However, professional advice is still required when drafting an object or powers, since the new rules are full of technical traps for the unwary. Whether modern or not, before a company enters into any new or unusual transaction, the objects and powers must be checked and, if necessary, legal advice sought, to ensure that they cover the proposed transaction. Whilst this is now less common, a bank may occasionally request a copy of the company's memorandum if money is borrowed by the company. It will make its own check on the company's objects and powers to ensure that it can borrow money, and, if appropriate, create mortgages and give guarantees. If it is not satisfied with the company's objects and powers, it may require the shareholders of the company to change them before it will lend money to the company. In any event, a company should ensure that its objects and powers are reviewed periodically by its professional advisers, to ensure that it continues to cover the company's activities – say every 2 years, and certainly upon the introduction of new legislation affecting companies.

A company may change its objects and powers by special resolution of its shareholders. Any change takes effect immediately upon passing of the resolution.

Within 15 days of the resolution being passed, a copy of it, and a reprint of the memorandum showing the changes must be lodged with the registrar of companies.

Statement of liability

The memorandum of every company must state that the liability of the shareholders of the company is limited. A prospective company which does not have such a statement in its memorandum will be refused registration.

This clause cannot be changed unless the company re-registers as an unlimited liability company which is a very unusual type of company.

Authorised share capital

Every company is required to state in its memorandum the amount of its authorised share capital. Authorised share capital is sometimes called nominal capital. The amount of the company's initial authorised share capital should be sufficient to enable the company to sell shares to raise the money it needs to carry on business in the future. For example, if it is anticipated that a company will need £1,000, after borrowing, in order to carry on business, it should have an authorised share capital of at least £1,000. Of course, it will be easier for the company to sell 1,000 shares of £1 each than say four shares of £250 each, so shares are usually 'denominated' as £1 shares.

A company may be incorporated with an authorised share capital of an amount which is greater than the amount it needs to raise for its initial working capital. After issuing sufficient shares to satisfy that need, it will have a number of unissued shares, which the directors can hold in reserve for some future issue. This means that they will be able to make future issues without going back to the shareholders and asking them to increase the authorised share capital to create more shares.

This may be appropriate if the company knows that it may need to issue more shares in the future – for example, if it has granted options to its directors or employees whereby they are entitled to buy the company's shares in the future, the company may retain sufficient unissued shares in its authorised capital to enable those options to be satisfied when they are exercised.

The statement must also state the number of shares in the authorised share capital, and the nominal (or par) value of each share. Although the nominal value of each share is usually £1, it may be any figure. Some shares may be of one nominal value and others of another, but this is unusual. The importance of the nominal value of a share is that no share may be sold by the company for less than its nominal value.

Payment for a share need not be made immediately. It may be deferred for as long as the company and shareholder agree. However, most private companies require immediate payment when they sell the shares. If the company and the shareholder agree, payment may also be made in any currency in an amount calculated according to the exchange rate at the date of payment.

A company's share capital does not need to be in pounds sterling. It may be denominated in any currency. However, once a share has been issued, it cannot be changed to a nominal value in another currency. The company's annual accounts need not be prepared in the currency of the company's share capital.

The authorised share capital of the company may be sold by the company until it is exhausted. A share sold by a company is said to be issued, or allotted. Directors usually deal with the issue of shares. If further authorised share capital is required, the directors must ask the company's shareholders to increase the authorised share capital by a further sum, and specify the number and nominal value of the new shares. This is done by ordinary resolution.

A copy of this resolution must be lodged with the registrar of companies, together with an official form, within 15 days after it is passed.

A private company may operate with only one share in issue – the minimum number required by law. There is no need to issue all of the authorised share capital, or even a major proportion of it, provided at least one share has been issued. However, for historical reasons, most private companies are formed with at least two shares issued from the outset, even if the company is intended to operate as a single member company. The same is not true of public companies which must be formed with an issued capital of at least two shares, and may not trade or borrow money unless the registrar of companies has certified that they have a minimum issued share capital of £50,000. See Chapter 1 in this respect. A company may have an authorised share capital divided into classes.

Up to four persons may buy a share jointly. It is the first named in the company's register of shareholders who will be entitled to receive notices, dividends, etc, in respect of the jointly held share, so the secretary of the company must be sure that the register is made up in accordance with the wishes of the joint shareholders.

The articles of association and Table A ***

The memorandum and articles are two quite separate documents, even though they are usually bound together.

The articles of association of the company are its rules and regulations. The contents of the articles are decided by the shareholders. The articles fix the manner in which the directors and shareholders of the company are to act, both amongst themselves and in relation to each other. Technically, the articles are treated as a contract between each shareholder and the company, so that breach of the articles may be treated as a breach of contract. Of course, matters which are already regulated by the Companies Acts do not need to be dealt with in the articles.

For example, the Companies Acts say that a company may not change its name without a special resolution of the shareholders. Changes to a company's name do not therefore need to be regulated by the articles. However, matters not dealt with by the Companies Acts may be regulated by the articles.

If a company does not lodge articles with the registrar of companies, Table A applies as if it were the articles of the company. Table A is a model set of articles. Its contents are decided by the Secretary of State for Trade and Industry. A copy of the current Table A for companies incorporated in Great Britain appears at Appendix C. The Table A for Northern Ireland is virtually identical.

However, Table A is very widely drafted. Shareholders of most companies will not want every provision of Table A to apply. They will want to make alterations and additions to Table A, to suit their particular needs and circumstances. The Companies Acts allow shareholders of a company to do this.

One way of doing this is to file with the registrar a set of articles which say that Table A shall not apply to the company at all. A company may then file articles which completely replace Table A with regulations acceptable to its shareholders.

However, most companies will find that Table A is largely satisfactory, and that only a few changes to it are necessary. It is therefore customary to file articles which begin with a clause which says that Table A applies 'except as follows'. There then follows a set of articles which vary or exclude certain provisions of Table A from applying. The rest of Table A continues to apply. The vast majority of companies do this.

Directors and shareholders of companies with articles drafted in this way will need to cross-refer from their articles to Table A. Most companies have a copy of Table A bound into the back of the articles so that it is easy to cross-refer. If not, copies of Table A are available from the Stationery Office for a small fee.

A company's first articles are usually lodged, with the other formation details with the registrar of companies.

A company may alter its articles, or adopt a whole new set, by special resolution of the shareholders. A copy of the altered or new articles must be filed with the registrar of companies within 15 days after the alteration or adoption. A company need not file a copy of Table A.

Great care should be taken when cross-referring from a company's articles to Table A. This is because there have been around a dozen different versions of Table A; which applies to a particular company will depend upon the circumstances. As a general rule, any Table A which originally applied to the company when it was formed will continue to apply, no matter how old the company is, or how many subsequent versions of Table A have been introduced since, unless the company specifically decides otherwise by a special resolution of the shareholders. If in any doubt, take professional advice.

It is good practice to ensure that articles of association are reviewed by professional advisers periodically – say every two years and certainly upon the introduction of new legislation affecting companies. There may be very good reasons for altering the articles or adopting new articles, to take advantage of powers under new legislation and case-law, and to take account of current business practice.

Some of the matters ordinarily dealt with in articles are:

(1)   the manner in which shares are to be issued;
(2)   the manner in which shares may be transferred;
(3)   the manner in which notices are given to and by the company;
(4)   directors' powers to vote on matters in which they have a personal interest;

(5)   the circumstances in which directors must vacate office, or may be removed;

(6)   the extent to which directors and other officers of the company may be indemnified by the company if they make mistakes;

(7)   the chairman's casting vote.

The articles provide a balance between the shareholders and the directors. Shareholders could provide in the articles that they must take every decision themselves, but ordinarily they will delegate as much of the day-to-day running of the business of the company to the directors as they can.

For matters which they cannot delegate, see Chapter 15.

The first directors and secretary, and intended situation of registered office

The Companies Acts require that, for a company to be formed, Companies House must be sent details of the proposed directors and secretary, and the intended situation of the registered office. For the rules governing the directors and secretary of a company, see Chapter 5.

The registered office of a company is merely an address for service of legal documents. It may be an accommodation address, although it must not be a post office box number. Often it is the address of the company's auditors or solicitors. The company does not need to carry on any trading activity from its registered office address, but it must keep certain of its registers there for inspection by the public. The address must appear on all business letters and order forms of the company.

Whatever the registered office address, the company must be sure that documents delivered to the company at that address will quickly come to the attention of the company's directors. The sort of documents served on the registered office will be writs, summonses, planning notices, and letters from the registrar of companies, threatening to strike the company from his index for failure to file returns.

If the registered office address is to be the home of a director, the secretary or a shareholder of the company, the homeowner must be very careful. There might be legal constraints on using his home for business purposes. These could be as a result of:

(1)   restrictive covenants in his title to the property, prohibiting business use;

(2)   restrictions on business use in his mortgage;

(3)   planning restrictions;

(4)   his capital gains tax position if his home is being used partly for business purposes;

(5)   his liability to local taxation.

Whilst he may argue that there is no business activity being carried on from his home, professional advice should be sought in each case.

Upon issue of the certificate of incorporation of a company, a person who has consented to act as a director in the information submitted to Companies House on the application for incorporation is automatically constituted a director of the company – no appointment or confirmation of his appointment is required after incorporation.

Formation procedure **

The incorporation procedure in the UK is much simpler and cheaper than in most other European countries. A solicitor, accountant or company registration agent will incorporate a new company within days. Ordinarily, all he requires is:

(1)   the official form duly completed; and
(2)   instructions on the proposed name, objects, authorised share capital, and various matters related to the contents of the articles.

The solicitor, accountant or agent, will do the rest, including name checking and providing subscribers.

If the solicitor, accountant or agent has formation software that has been approved by Companies House, and is registered with Companies House as an approved presenter, the formation details can be filed electronically. Companies House usually form companies filed electronically within 24 hours – usually far quicker than formations filed using paper forms.

Same-day incorporation **

In England and Wales or Scotland, it is possible to speed the whole incorporation procedure up, so that a company may be incorporated on the same day as the documents are filed. Additional requirements for a same-day incorporation are payment of an extra fee to Companies House, choice of a name for the company which does not contain a sensitive word, and ensuring that the incorporation documents are lodged before 3 pm on the proposed day of incorporation.

Same-day incorporations are not possible in Northern Ireland.

Ready-made companies **

It is also possible to acquire what are called 'ready-made', 'off the-shelf' or 'off-the-peg' companies, whether private or public. These are companies which have already been incorporated, but have carried on no activity whatsoever. Many solicitors and accountants carry stocks of such companies. Company registration agents certainly do. The companies are incorporated with neutral names, wide objects, standard articles, and, normally, an authorised share capital of £1,000. The subscribers and first director and secretary are employees or nominees of the solicitor, accountant or registration agents, and the registered office will be one of their trading addresses.

Upon signature of official forms by the proposed new directors and secretary in which they consent to act, and notification of new registered office address, and upon payment of a fee, the ready-made company is transferred over. If it is a private company, it is ready to trade immediately. If required, changes will be made to the company before it is transferred, such as changes to the name, authorised share capital, objects and articles – all except the change of name will take effect immediately. However, the change of name only takes effect once the appropriate shareholder resolution has been submitted to the registrar and he has issued a certificate of incorporation on change of name. It is therefore possible to acquire a private company which is ready to start trading in under half an hour, even though the company initially has a 'ready-made' name. However, same-day changes of name are possible, as discussed below. Care must always be taken to ensure that the company has not carried on any activity at all whilst it was a ready-made company. The company papers should include a certificate or declaration that the company has not traded.

Whilst a private company is able to trade with immediate effect from the date of issue of the certificate of incorporation, a public company is required to obtain a further certificate, commonly called a trading certificate, before it may trade or borrow money.

A solicitor, accountant or company registration agent will advise as to the procedure to obtain a trading certificate. The certificate of incorporation is conclusive evidence that all the requirements of the Companies Acts relating to incorporation have been complied with.

Same-day changes of name **

Whilst the name of a ready-made company cannot be changed immediately, it can be changed on a same-day basis. As with a same-day incorporation, payment of an additional fee to Companies House, choice of a new company name which does not contain a sensitive word and ensuring that the documents to change the name are lodged before 3 pm will procure a change of name on the same day.

As with same-day incorporation, same-day changes of name are only possible in England and Wales or Scotland. They are not possible in Northern Ireland.

Who will need a copy of the memorandum and articles?

A company usually has eight copies of its memorandum and articles. All or any of the following may want a copy:

(1)   the auditor or other accountant to the company;
(2)   the solicitor;
(3)   the bank;
(4)   the Inland Revenue;
(5)   the company secretary;
(6)   each director;
(7)   each shareholder.

Registers *

A private company *must* keep the following registers:

(1)   register of directors;
(2)   register of secretaries;
(3)   register of shareholders;
(4)   register of directors' interests in shares;
(5)   register of charges (mortgages).

All of these are open to public inspection, although the company may charge a (very small) fee in certain circumstances, for making them available. Invariably, this fee is waived.

It will usually also keep a register of applications for and allotments of shares, a register of share transfers, and a register of dealings, but these are not required under the Companies Acts, and are not open to public inspection.

Filing requirements

Many transactions or events generate a requirement to file a document or statutory form at Companies House within a certain time-limit. The time-limit varies according to the transaction or event. In a few cases, the validity of the transaction or event is dependent on the filing. The filing requirements relating to the transactions and events covered by this book are dealt with in the text. However, for an exhaustive list of filing requirements and statutory forms in an accessible format, *Reminders for Company Secretaries* (Jordans, 1997) and other Jordans publications should be consulted.

Whichever document or form is being filed, the registry will microfilm it for the company's public file, which means that it must be capable of being identified as relevant to the company and capable of being read when the microfilm is magnified. The following registry guidelines should be observed:

(1)   use black ink or type;
(2)   use bold lettering;
(3)   do not file carbon copies;
(4)   do not use dot matrix printers to produce documents for filing;
(5)   remember that photocopies will result in grey shades which do not transfer well to microfilm records;
(6)   always include the company number in a prominent position on the first page, preferably top right-hand corner;
(7)   ensure pages are white A4, with a matt finish;
(8)   margins should not be less than 10 mm or, if the document is bound, 20 mm;
(9)   letters and numbers should not be less than 1.8 mm high, and should have a line width of not less than 0.25 mm.

However, certain information can be filed electronically rather than on paper forms. At the time of writing, information about officers – new appointments, changes in particulars like addresses, and notification of cessation of office – can be made via www.companieshouse.gov.uk. Alternatively, your solicitor, accountant or the company secretary may have bought company secretarial software that enables him to file information electronically.

Currently, the information that can be filed electronically is fairly limited, but Companies House is committed both to extending the range of information that can be filed electronically, and making electronic filing more accessible.

First board meeting *

It is clear that a company need not carry on a business for days, months – even years after its incorporation. Some companies are incorporated solely in order to protect a name, and never carry on a business. See Chapter 1 for the rules as to such dormant companies.

However, before a company starts trading, it will ordinarily want to deal with certain administrative matters. For example, it would be unusual if the company did not wish to open a bank account before trading. The professional adviser or company registration agent should provide an agenda and specimen minutes for a meeting of the board of directors at which these administrative matters may be dealt with.

CHAPTER 3

Shares and Shareholders in a Private Company

Shares

As has been seen, the basic structure of a company is that shareholders put money in by buying shares, and then appoint directors who manage the business on behalf of the company.

Shares give shareholders rights which are usually set out in the articles. Lawyers will often describe a share as 'a bundle of rights'.

Most companies have one class of share only. Usually all shares have equal rights. Share rights will usually cover the right to vote at shareholders' meetings, the right to a dividend if there are sufficient profits, the right to divide the company's surplus money (once it has sold all its property, paid its debts and discharged its liabilities) among themselves if it is wound up, and equal rights with other shareholders on issue or transfer of all shares.

Shareholders

Any person can be a shareholder, whether an individual or a company, and irrespective of nationality, age or tax status. Persons under 18 years old may be shareholders, although this can have awkward consequences upon sale of the shares. Advice should be taken if this is intended. More usually, shares are held by trustees in trust for the benefit of those aged under 18. However, a company may restrict who is able to own its shares in its articles, so that the articles of each company should always be checked to see if they contain any provision restricting who may be a shareholder. Shareholders of a company are sometimes called 'members' of the company.

A private company may be formed either with two or more shareholders or with one shareholder. A private company with one shareholder is known as a single member company and is subject to additional rules that do not apply to multi-member companies (see p 38).

In contrast, a public company should never have only one shareholder. If it does, and carries on trading for more than 6 months, the sole shareholder will, if he knows he is the sole shareholder, become personally liable, jointly and severally with the company, for payment of the company's debts incurred after that 6-month period. In other words, a sole shareholder loses limited liability.

Single member companies ***

A single member company is subject to special rules.

(1)   It must include a note stating that it is a single member company against the name of the single member in the register of members, and of the date it became a single member company. Upon ceasing to be a single member company, a note of this fact, and the date of ceasing to be a single member company must also be made.

(2)   If the single member is also a director, it must record in writing all contracts entered into between the company and the single member company, other than those entered into in the ordinary course of business.

(3)   All informal decisions of the single member not recorded as minutes of a meeting of the single member or as a resolution in writing in lieu of a meeting, must be recorded in writing.

The articles of association of a company which is to operate as a single member company may need to contain special provisions – this is particularly the case if the single member is also to be the sole director of the company. In that instance, the question of how the member's shares will transmit under his will or intestacy must be dealt with if the company is not to grind to a complete halt on the single member's death. If, as will often be the case in a private company, the articles say that the deceased member's personal representatives are unable to transfer his shares to, for example, the beneficiaries under his will without consent of the directors but, as a result of the death, the company is without any directors, a lacuna occurs. Ordinarily, personal representatives of a deceased member have no right to vote at general meetings. However, to avoid this lacuna, in the event of the death of a sole member who was also the sole director, but in no other circumstances, it is prudent to have articles which allow the personal representatives to appoint a new director or directors, but confer no other power to vote. The new board may then deal with any application to transfer shares submitted by the personal representatives in the usual way.

The rule against a sole director also being the secretary continues to apply to single member companies with a sole director – whilst one person may be the single member and the sole director, another person must act as secretary.

Issuing shares **

Professional advice will be required in respect of every aspect of issuing shares – the company should involve the adviser at the very outset. The following paragraphs provide an indication of some important considerations. It must be recognised that the duties of directors (to always act in good faith in what they honestly believe to be in the best interests of the company, and for proper purposes – see Chapter 5) are particularly important when the directors propose to issue shares. Shares are not, for example, tools whereby a majority shareholder ensures that his company remains under his control. Instead, they must only be issued if it is in the best interests of the company that they be issued.

Shares may be issued for cash (see Figure 6), or non-cash payment, including services, but they must never be issued 'at a discount'. This means that they cannot be issued for less than their nominal value. They may be issued at a premium. A premium is a sum over and above the nominal value of the share. For example, a company which is about to pay a big dividend might find that someone is willing to buy its £1 shares for more than £1. If so, it will issue the share at a premium. It is up to the company and the shareholder to agree the price for the shares, and when the shares will be paid for. However, it is unusual to find shares in a private company which are not paid for in full (including any premium) immediately on issue. Shares which have been paid for in full are called 'fully-paid shares'. Shares which have not been paid for will be either 'nil-paid shares' or 'partly-paid shares'.

Of course, before shares may be issued, the company must have sufficient unissued shares in its authorised share capital. If it does not, it will need to increase its authorised share capital by ordinary resolution of shareholders. A shareholders' meeting may need to be called to deal with this.

Issuing shares is so important to shareholders that the Companies Acts say that the issue of shares must be expressly delegated to directors by the shareholders.

For the directors to issue shares, they must therefore have an express authority to do so from the shareholders. Often the authority is in the articles, but it may also be given by ordinary resolution of the shareholders. Legal advice should always include confirmation that the directors are authorised by the shareholders to deal with the issue of shares, whether in the articles, or by ordinary resolution. If the directors do not have such an authority, a shareholders' meeting may need to be called to give them this authority.

Once the directors of the company are sure that they have authority to issue shares from the shareholders, they must check to see whether they are required to issue those shares in any special way. For example, the Companies Acts, or the company's articles, or a mixture of both, may state that the directors cannot issue shares to whoever they want. Often they must first offer them to existing shareholders in proportion to the number of shares held by them. Such rights in favour of existing shareholders are called 'pre-emption rights'.

Whatever the case, the provisions of the articles, or the Acts, or a combination of the two, must be strictly observed. Professional advice will always be required.

Shares are usually issued for cash payment. If they are offered to the existing shareholders, in proportion to their existing shares in return for cash, the issue is called a 'rights issue'.

Almost as common is a 'bonus issue'. This is sometimes called a 'scrip issue' or a 'capitalisation'. The last is the most accurate description.

A bonus issue occurs when a company has built up profits and reserves. Instead of paying the profits out as dividend, the shareholders are offered new shares in the company, on the basis that the shareholder need not pay for them. The profits which have built up in the company will be used to pay for the shares.

On a bonus issue of 1,000 shares of £1 the company's balance sheet will alter from this:

issued share capital	£1,000
profit and loss account	£1,000

to this:

issued share capital	£2,000
profit and loss account	nil

The company benefits in that it keeps the money, as capital, rather than having to pay it out as dividend, and the shareholders benefit in that they acquire shares without having to find the money to pay for them. In effect, profits have been 'capitalised' into share capital.

In fact, it is not only profits, but also share premium account, capital redemption reserve and revaluation reserve which may be used to pay for a bonus issue.

However, the procedural and tax aspects of a bonus issue mean that professional advice is particularly important.

Whilst not directly relevant to the types of company contemplated by this book, mention needs to be made here of the practice of many Stock Exchange companies of offering 'scrip dividends'. A scrip dividend occurs when shareholders of a company are offered the option to subscribe for further shares in the company, without payment, of a value equivalent to the value of all, or part of a dividend which the company will otherwise pay to them. Whilst there are similarities between a bonus issue and a scrip dividend, the two are, in fact, quite different transactions.

It is also quite possible for shares to be issued in return for a non-cash payment. An example of this is the sale to a company of a business formerly carried on by partners in return for shares in the company.

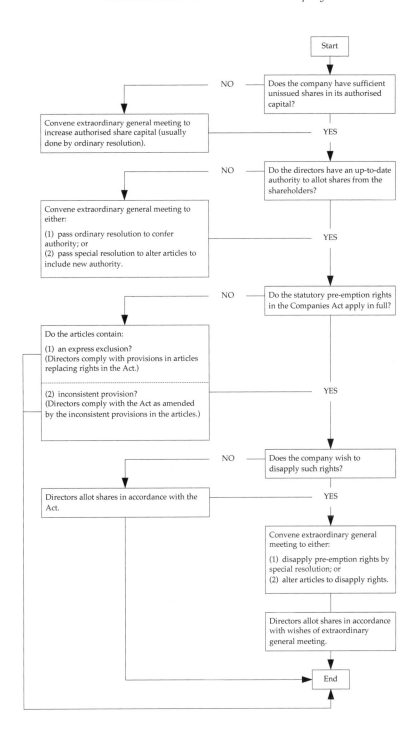

Figure 6 – Issue of shares for cash

Shares are sometimes offered to existing shareholders on 'renounceable letters of allotment'. This means that a shareholder is given the option of asking the company to issue the shares not to him but to some other person. He does this by completing part of the letter of allotment accordingly, and asking the other person to complete the remainder of it, for return to the company within the time-limit for accepting the offer.

A 'renunciation' of shares is treated for some purposes as if it were a transfer of shares by the shareholder to another person, so that for example, the company's transfer articles, or prohibitions on transfer in a shareholders' agreement will apply.

If a shareholder does renounce shares to another person, the name of that other person will go straight into the company's registers, and on the official form (Return of Allotments) filed with Companies House when the shares are issued.

Special rules apply for shares issued under an employee share option scheme.

Every time new shares are issued, the registrar of companies must be told, and, if the payment for the shares is not cash, stamp duty may be payable by the company on the property transferred to it. The company's professional adviser will deal with this aspect.

Registers and disclosure **

Every time a share is issued, it is vital to make the necessary entries in the company's registers. The register of shareholders (or members) is the most important register since it is evidence of the identity of the shareholders of the company. This register is open to public inspection.

It may also be necessary to update the register of directors' interests in shares of the company. If a director is directly or indirectly interested in the issue of shares (for example, he or a member of his family is buying them) this should be disclosed in advance at a meeting of the directors.

In unusual circumstances, where shares are issued to a director or a person connected with him, and the company is receiving a non-cash payment of a substantial value, the transaction may need to be approved by the shareholders in general meeting before it may go ahead. Such a transaction is called 'a substantial property transaction involving directors'. These rules were introduced to stop rogue directors buying assets from their company at an undervalue or selling assets to their company at an overvalue. However, they sometimes also apply when, for example, two or more partners transfer their business to a company, which they have set up for the purpose. In return the company issues them with shares. If they are directors, and the partnership business is large enough, this may be a substantial property transaction. The company's professional adviser will ensure that the procedural requirements are dealt with.

Share certificates *

Every time shares are issued, the company should issue share certificates within 2 months, to the holders of the new issued shares. Share certificates should be properly executed in accordance with the articles and the companies legislation of each of England and Wales, Scotland or Northern Ireland. Prior to the rules introduced in 1989 and 1990 respectively, share certificates of English and Northern Irish companies always had to be sealed. Now companies do not have to have a seal. If the company has a seal, and decides to use it in respect of the share certificates, English and Northern Irish law requires that the certificates should be sealed and the seal countersigned in accordance with the company's articles. Otherwise the new methods of execution introduced for companies which opt not to have a common seal or, if they have one, opt not to use it, should be followed which always require the signatures of two officers. Scottish law has never required share certificates to be sealed, so they may simply be signed by two signatories, each of whom may be either an officer or an authorised person. However, advice should always be sought in relation to execution of documents under Scottish laws as the difficulties inherent in this complex area of law have been compounded by inadequate legislative drafting and consequent repeal and re-enactment of the rules. Not only are the rules complex but the current version of them is hard to find!

Classes of share **

It is often appropriate to have two or more different classes of share. Each class of share will carry different rights. Such rights are normally set out in the company's articles, but they need not be (unless they are rights to redeem the shares in which case they must appear in the articles). Wherever they are set out, they must appear on the company's public record at Companies House. If they are in the articles, they will appear at Companies House in any event. If not, they must be set out on an official form, which is filed instead.

A company will ordinarily start out with only one class of share. These will carry equal rights to vote at shareholders' meetings, and a right to receive a dividend if the company has enough profit to pay one. On a winding up, each share will carry the right to a portion of any money left over after the company has paid off the costs of the winding up and any other debts and liabilities it has. The more shares a shareholder has bought, the more votes, dividend and money in a winding up he will be entitled to. He is being rewarded for having put his money into the company by buying its shares. Often there will be a requirement that, on issue of new shares, or transfer of shares already in issue, such shares must be offered to the existing shareholders, in proportion to their respective shareholdings. These rights on issue and transfer are also rights attaching to shares.

There may come a stage when it is appropriate for the company to create a second or third class of share. For example, the company may wish to raise a great deal of money very quickly, to take advantage of a business opportunity, or to sustain an anticipated growth in its business. In those circumstances, a venture capitalist may agree to provide the money. A venture capitalist is an organisation which makes a business of investing money, usually in companies carrying on a relatively small business but with bright prospects. Of course, the investment is often a risky one, so the venture capitalist will want to negotiate a good return on the investment. The venture capitalist will usually lend money to the company, and also buy its shares. A second, and sometimes a third, class of share is usually created for the venture capitalist. Venture Capital Trusts have also made such investments more attractive for the private investor.

Alternatively, a company may wish to reward its employees for their hard work. However, the existing shareholders will not wish to dilute their voting power – their control of the company. A second class of share for the employees is the answer.

Shareholders of the company will often want members of their family to hold shares in their company so they may enjoy dividends. Often such shares are for younger members of the family – who are too young to have much commercial judgment. In such circumstances, the shares might be held on trust for the youngsters. It would be imprudent to allow such shareholders too much voting power, so a new class of share is created.

The rights, and, indeed, restrictions, which could be attached to the second class of share in each case are set out below. Of course, these rights will not be appropriate in every case, and nor are they exhaustive. Professional advice will always be needed.

Class rights for the venture capitalist

(1) To block any change in the company's authorised or issued share capital;
(2) to a dividend in preference to the holders of any other class, up to a specified amount (often a percentage of the nominal value of each share in the class);
(3) to a further dividend, equally with the other class of share;
(4) to carry forward the right to a dividend if it is not paid in a particular year (a cumulative dividend);
(5) to vote, but only if the cumulative dividend is not paid, or the company wishes to do something major, such as alter its objects or wind itself up;
(6) to redeem its shares – to cash them in and get its money back. The articles usually provide for this to happen on a fixed date, or earlier, in certain circumstances;
(7) to preferential rights to surplus money if the company is wound up;
(8) to appoint a director in certain circumstances;
(9) to convert their shares into shares of a different class;
(10) to transfer their shares to other organisations in the same group as the venture capitalist.

Class rights for employees

(1) Not to vote in any circumstances, or to vote, but only in matters relating to employees;
(2) to dividends, equally with other classes of share;
(3) to transfer freely to members of their family, or to trustees of trusts for the benefit of members of their family; otherwise to transfer only in restricted circumstances;
(4) to offer the shares back to other members, employees and their families, on cessation of employment, whether through resignation, bankruptcy or death.

Great care must be taken with employee shares. Tax benefits may be available on purchase and sale of shares, and options to buy shares by employees, if a share scheme is set up which meets the criteria for Inland Revenue approval. Professional advice is vital if such a scheme is contemplated.

Class rights for the family

(1) Not to vote in any circumstances;
(2) to dividends, equally with other classes of share;
(3) to transfer freely to other members of the family, or to trustees of trusts for the benefit of members of their family, or to members of the family on death. Otherwise to transfer only in restricted circumstances.

Once rights have been attached to shares, they cannot be varied or altered without the consent of the holders of the shares carrying those rights. Ordinarily the consent of the holders of three-quarters in nominal value of the class shares is sufficient consent.

Subject to this, share rights which appear in the articles may be altered by special resolution of the shareholders of the company.

It is possible to entrench share rights so that they cannot be altered at all. However, this is dangerous, and should only be done after careful thought and professional advice.

Redemption, repurchase by a company of its shares and reductions in share capital ***

Once a shareholder has paid for his shares, he cannot usually ask the company to repay his money unless the company is wound up. He cannot 'cash his shares in'. However, there are three special circumstances in which he can get his money back.

Redemption of shares

First, the shares might be issued as redeemable shares. On redemption the shareholder gets his money back, and the redeemed shares are cancelled. The terms of redemption – when it is to occur, how much the shareholder gets back – should be set out in the articles. Shares cannot be converted into redeemable shares after issue – they must be issued as redeemable shares. The shareholder must know from the outset that his shares may be redeemed and the terms upon which this will happen.

Redemption may occur at a fixed time, or at the option of the company, or of the shareholder, or both. There may be a 'long-stop date' by which redemption must take place in any event. Ordinarily, not all the redeemable shares have to be redeemed at the same time.

Redeemable shares are a useful way of attracting investors who wish to hold shares for a specific time – like a venture capitalist. Once that time has elapsed, the venture capitalist knows it will get its money back, and the company knows, for cash flow purposes, when it will need to make funds available.

A company should not issue or redeem redeemable shares without professional advice.

Repurchase by company of its own shares

Secondly, the company might buy its own shares back. As with a redemption, the shareholder gets his money back and the shares bought back are cancelled. The difference between a purchase and a redemption is that the terms of the purchase are agreed between the shareholder and the company at the time of the purchase, whereas the terms of redemption are fixed at the time of issue of the shares.

A purchase of its own shares can be a very useful way of persuading an awkward shareholder to relinquish his shares, or providing a retiring shareholder with a nest-egg for retirement when he can find no other buyer for his shares.

However, no purchase of own shares should take place without professional advice.

It is important to note that neither a redemption nor a purchase of own shares is carried out as a simple transfer of shares. There are specific procedures to be observed in each case.

Reduction of share capital

Thirdly, a company may reduce its issued share capital by a special resolution, sanctioned by a court order. This is an unusual procedure, rarely used by private companies.

Financial assistance ***

A purchase of its own shares by a company should be distinguished from a transaction which lawyers call 'financial assistance'. Financial assistance occurs when a company provides cash or some other help from its own resources to allow someone to buy its shares. A common example is where company A buys shares in company B. Company A borrows money from the bank to do this. Company B creates a mortgage over its property in the bank's favour as security for the borrowing. Company B is clearly giving financial assistance to company A to allow it to buy company B's shares.

Of course, there are many other examples. Companies are not allowed to give financial assistance without going through a special procedure. Professional advice will always be required.

One exception from the rules on financial assistance is a bonus issue. A company which issues new shares to its shareholders, but pays them up itself, from its profits, would be giving financial assistance were it not for the fact that the Companies Acts specifically exclude bonus issues from the special procedure.

Transfer of shares **

Transfer of shares which are already in existence should be distinguished from an issue of new shares. Shareholders have a free right to transfer their shares, subject to any restrictions which they might agree to impose on themselves. Such restrictions usually appear in the company's articles, or in a shareholders' agreement. Almost all private companies will have some sort of restriction, although it will vary from company to company.

Most companies simply provide that a shareholder may only transfer a share if the directors of the company approve the transfer. Directors do not usually need to give reasons for any refusal.

Another common restriction is to say that a share may not be transferred unless it is offered to the other shareholders first. In this circumstance it is usual to provide that, if necessary, the shares are to be valued by an independent expert. This can prove costly – it is difficult to value a private company's shares – so that an independent valuation should only be used as a last resort. There may be circumstances in which shareholders want to be free to transfer shares, without the directors' consent, and without having to offer them to the other shareholders. A free transfer of this type is commonly allowed in family companies. Shareholders are given a free right to transfer shares to members of their family, or to trustees of a trust set up for the benefit of members of their family.

Of course, it is possible to combine these options. Shareholders might be given a free right to transfer to family members, family trustees, etc, but are required to precede an offer of their shares to any other person by an offer of those shares to the other members.

These are just some of the most common options – the possibilities are endless. All too often, insufficient thought is given to the transfer of shares. At the beginning of the company's life, the furthest thought from a shareholder's mind is the sale of his shares. A good professional adviser will always raise the question of transfer, and it should be given careful consideration (see Figure 7).

It is easy to make mistakes without proper advice. A common problem arises when a majority shareholder, who is obliged to offer his shares to other shareholders under the articles, finds that the other shareholders are permitted to accept only some of his shares. He is then left with a minority holding, of greatly reduced value to a purchaser, which he cannot get rid of. A professional adviser will raise issues of this sort, and advise on a solution, such as requiring the other shareholders to accept all the shares before the vendor shareholder is obliged to sell to them.

Bankruptcy or death of a shareholder **

So far, reference has been made to the transfer of shares, by a shareholder who is alive and solvent. Shareholders do, of course, die, and go bankrupt. In such circumstances, an event occurs which is called 'transmission'. It is automatic.

Death of a shareholder – law of England and Wales and of Northern Ireland

Dealing first with death of a shareholder under the laws of England and Wales or Northern Ireland, a shareholder who dies may leave a will, or he may die without making a will. If he dies without making a will, he is said to die 'intestate'.

A shareholder who has left a will should have named the person or persons whom he wishes to look after his property, including his shares, after his death. The will may require them either to pass his property to his heirs, sell it and give them the money, or a mixture of both. Such a person is called an 'executor' or, if female, an 'executrix'. The executors of the shareholder will apply to the High Court for a document to prove that they are executors and therefore entitled to deal with the shareholder's property. This document is called a 'grant of probate' or 'probate' for short. When dealing with the shareholders' property, the executors are said to 'administer his estate'.

If the shareholder dies intestate, he will not have said whom he wishes to look after his property, or what is to be done with it. In these circumstances the law allows his nearest relatives to look after his property – to 'administer his estate' – and specifies who is to inherit his estate. Such persons are called 'administrators' and the document which they apply for at the High Court is called 'letters of administration'.

The law uses the expression 'personal representatives' to cover both executors and administrators – it is this expression which will appear in any articles or shareholders' agreement.

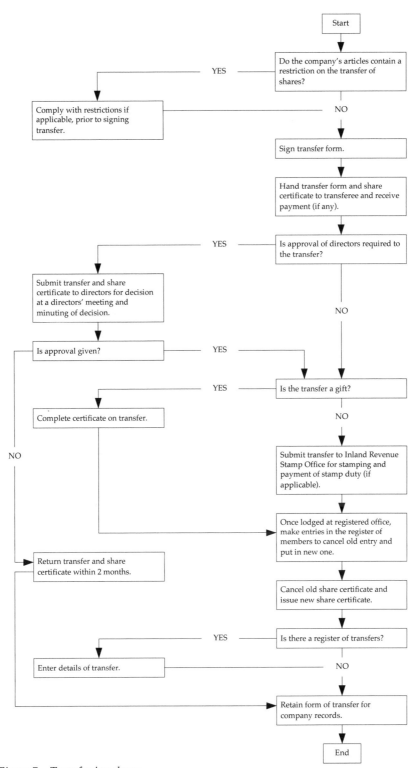

Figure 7 – Transferring shares

The effect of the death of a shareholder is usually that the company recognises his personal representatives as the persons entitled to his shares. This recognition is automatic and is called 'transmission'. Of course, the company will need to see the probate or letters of administration, stating the names of the personal representatives, before it will recognise them. However, being recognised as entitled to shares does not make the personal representatives full shareholders of the company. The practical consequence is that the name of the deceased shareholder stays in the register of shareholders despite the death, and the secretary merely inserts the names and addresses of the personal representatives as a note in the register.

They do have certain rights. For example, they are entitled to have dividends sent to them, if declared, and to be offered shares on any bonus or rights issue. Dividends or shares received in this way do not belong to the personal representatives. They are added to the deceased shareholder's property and dealt with as if owned by the shareholder when he died.

However, personal representatives are not usually entitled to exercise the voting rights attaching to the shares of the deceased shareholder. For voting purposes, the deceased's shares are held in limbo.

One of two things may then happen. The personal representatives may decide that they want to become full shareholders in respect of the shares themselves. If so, they are said to 'elect' to become shareholders. Alternatively, they may wish to transfer the shares to someone else, who will become a full member. However, most companies will provide in their articles that any election by personal representatives to become full shareholders, or any transfer by the personal representatives to a new shareholder, is to be treated as if it were a transfer by the shareholder who died. This means that any restrictions on transfer will apply.

For example, if the articles say that no transfer will take place without the shares first being offered to the other shareholders, the personal representatives must offer them to the other shareholders before making an election, or trying to transfer to a new shareholder.

Shareholders often fail to appreciate that the restrictions on transfer will override any provision in their will or in the rules as to who inherits on intestacy. A shareholder who leaves shares to a spouse or children in a will might be surprised to find that the directors of the company refuse to approve a transfer of those shares to the spouse and children by the personal representatives. However, this is quite possible. A shareholder who wishes to ensure that shares end up in the hands of his spouse and children must ensure that the articles of the company contain a free right of transfer of shares to members of the family. The personal representatives are then as free to transfer to the spouse and children as the shareholder himself would have been had he lived.

It is not until an election or transfer has been dealt with in accordance with the articles that the deceased shareholder ceases to appear as the owner of shares in the register of shareholders of the company.

Death of a shareholder – Scottish law

In the event of the bankruptcy or death of a Scottish shareholder of a limited company, whether the company is registered in Scotland, or in England and Wales, the provisions of Scottish law will apply to his property – including his shares in the limited company. These provisions are substantially different from those in England and Wales. In the event of bankruptcy or death, advice from a qualified Scottish professional is strongly recommended to anyone not familiar with Scottish law.

In the event of the death of a Scottish shareholder, if the deceased leaves a will which contains the appointment of executors, those appointed will apply to the appropriate Sheriff Court for their appointment as 'executors nominate'. If there is no appointment of executors in the will, or there is no will, the next of kin (or, in some cases, other persons) can petition the Sheriff Court for an order recognising them as 'executors-dative'. Thereafter the executors may obtain confirmation in their name to administer the estate. Although there are differences of procedure prior to such appointment, executors appointed in either circumstances are 'personal representatives' of the deceased to whom the comments above apply.

Bankruptcy of a shareholder – laws of England and Wales and of Northern Ireland

Much the same rules apply on bankruptcy of the shareholder under the laws of England and Wales and of Northern Ireland as on death. Once officially bankrupt, an official called a 'trustee in bankruptcy' becomes recognised as entitled to the bankrupt's shares. The term 'personal representative' also covers a trustee in bankruptcy, so that he can, subject to the articles, elect to become a full shareholder, or may wish to transfer the bankrupt's shares. Until he does one of these, he can receive dividends and shares on behalf of the bankrupt, but cannot vote with the bankrupt's shares.

Bankruptcy of a shareholder – Scottish law

In the case of a bankruptcy under Scottish law, an individual will be recognised as formally bankrupt if he signs a voluntary trust deed or is sequestrated by the court. The person appointed to act as his trustee in either case will be a recognised 'insolvency practitioner' and is generally referred to as the individual's 'trustee in bankruptcy'. Again, he will be treated by the company as the individual shareholder's 'personal representative'.

There are other similar situations in which the court may appoint a 'personal representative' to a shareholder. If he is incapable of managing his own affairs the appointment is of a *curator bonis*. If the estate of a deceased person is insolvent, a judicial factor may be appointed, but a judicial factor may also be appointed in circumstances apart from insolvency, such as where a partnership or even a limited company is unable effectively to manage its affairs as a result of some internal dispute. Generally speaking, all such appointments will be covered by the expression 'personal representative'.

Stamp duty on transfer of shares *

Stamp duty must be paid on a transfer of shares (but not an election), unless a relief or exemption is available. As with a house purchase, payment of any stamp duty is the buyer's responsibility. Stamp duty is calculated at £5 stamp duty for every £1,000 or part of £1,000, being received by the seller for the shares. There is a minimum sum payable of £5. Stamp duty calculated in this way is called 'ad valorem' duty.

However, there are circumstances where relief or exemption is available. The most common circumstance is a transfer by way of gift. Such a transfer is completely exempt from stamp duty, provided that the seller fills in an appropriate certificate stating that the exemption applies. Other transfers are not completely exempt but attract a fixed duty of only £5, provided, again, that an appropriate certificate is completed making it clear that only the fixed duty is payable. Circumstances in which those reliefs or exemptions are available, and the certificates which require completion if they are to be claimed, are usually pre-printed on the back of the stock transfer form.

However, there are other, less common, circumstances in which reliefs and exemptions may be available which are not referred to on the stock transfer form. These include reliefs available when, for example, one company 'takes over' another, or transfers of shares of and between companies in the same group take place. These transactions are complex and will always require professional advice and 'adjudication' by the Inland Revenue.

Procedure on transfer *

The procedure on transfer of shares in a private company by a living, solvent shareholder is as follows.

(1)   The buyer and seller check the articles of the company and any shareholders' agreement to see if any special provisions need to be observed before shares are transferred. For example, do the shares have to be offered to other shareholders before being transferred to the buyer? If so, any such requirement must be observed.
(2)   The seller completes a stock transfer form. The form must be signed by the seller, but if the share is fully paid it need not be signed by the buyer.
(3)   The seller hands the stock transfer form to the buyer, and receives payment, if any. The seller also hands over his share certificates relating to the shares. If he has lost them, the buyer may ask for

indemnity for the lost share certificates or insist that the seller obtains duplicates from the company. In the latter case, the company is likely to require an indemnity from the seller. Forms of indemnity are readily available in standard form from legal stationers.

(4) If the stamp duty is payable, the buyer is responsible for its payment, and should take advice as to the amount payable and whether reliefs or exemptions are available.

(5) The stock transfer form should be presented to the company. Prior to entering the transfer into the registers of the company, and issuing the new share certificates, the secretary will ensure that:

(a) the articles have been complied with. If the directors have power to refuse to register a transfer, they must exercise it within 2 months after the transfer form is presented to the company; and

(b) if stamp duty is relevant, that the stock transfer form is:
   (i)   either stamped with ad valorem duty; or
   (ii) stamped with £5 duty and a stamp showing it has been produced to the Stamp Office, and there is an appropriate certificate of relief; or
   (iii) the form has not been stamped at all but there is a certificate of exemption; or
   (iv) marked to indicate it has been 'adjudicated' by the Inland Revenue.

It is a criminal offence for the secretary to register a transfer if the stock transfer form has not been properly stamped and/or certified.

The secretary may then alter the registers, cancel or destroy old share certificates, and issue new ones. A shareholder must be given his new share certificate within 2 months after the transfer form is presented to the company. Not only will the register of shareholders require alteration, so may the register of directors' interests in shares, and, if the company has them, the register of transfers, and the register of sealings.

It is not necessary to inform Companies House of a transfer of shares when it occurs – details of transfers will, however, appear in the company's next annual return.

Shares held on trust **

It is possible to hold shares on trust. The shareholder may agree with another that he will deal with his shares in accordance with their instructions. The shareholder is then a 'trustee' and the other is a 'beneficiary'. There are many different sorts of trust, each of which give the beneficiary different rights.

For example, an accumulation and maintenance settlement is a complex form of trust used to benefit children.

The simplest form of trust is called, colloquially, a bare or, in Scotland sometimes, a simple, trust. It gives the beneficiary the right to direct the trustee as to how to deal with the shares held by the trustee in every respect, and requires the trustee to account to the beneficiary for dividends and other benefits received by the trustee in respect of the shares. The trustee is often called a 'nominee'. The beneficiary is often called a 'beneficial owner'. It is the name of the trustee which will appear in the company's registers and the annual return, so it is the trustee who is the shareholder. The company is not interested in any arrangement the shareholder has made and, ordinarily, its articles will provide that it will ignore the interests of the beneficiaries, even if the shareholder is merely a nominee under a bare trust. A private company will not ordinarily be able to find out the identity of the beneficial owner of any of its shares although, in certain circumstances, a public company may. In any event, even if the company knows about the beneficial owner, it takes note only of the shareholder. For example, if a beneficial owner of a share tells his nominee to vote for a resolution at a shareholders' meeting, and he votes against it, the company will not be interested in a complaint or objection by the beneficial owner. The beneficial owner's remedy is not to complain to the company, but to take the nominee to court for breach of the terms of the trust.

Wholly owned subsidiaries *

Bare trusts are often used in a group company structure. Often, every company in a group, except the ultimate parent company, will be a wholly owned subsidiary. This does *not* necessarily mean that every share in those companies is held by another company.

Instead, a common arrangement has traditionally been for all but one of the shares to be held by the immediate parent company, and the remaining share to be held by a nominee for the parent company on a bare trust. Under the stamp duty rules, the transfer of a share to such a nominee, or from one nominee to another, is a transfer which, if an appropriate certificate is given, is subject only to a fixed duty of £5. The parent company therefore has control over every share, but, because of the nominee, there are two shareholders in the subsidiary company's registers. The company is still a wholly owned subsidiary, because the Companies Acts define a 'wholly owned subsidiary' as a company whose shares are all held by another company, and that other company's nominees. This was because of a long-established rule that every company, even a wholly owned subsidiary, required two shareholders.

However, since the introduction of the rule that a private company may operate with a single shareholder without that single shareholder losing limited liability, the need for a nominee to hold a share in a private wholly owned subsidiary (so that there are two shareholders) has disappeared. All the shares in the subsidiary may now be registered in the name of the parent. Since most wholly owned subsidiaries are private companies, this applies to most wholly owned subsidiaries. However, in the rare instance of a subsidiary which is a public company, a nominee is still necessary.

The company is also a wholly owned subsidiary if all its shares are owned by another company and that other company is a wholly owned subsidiary.

Under the law of England and Wales and of Northern Ireland, a bare trust over shares need not be declared in writing, although it is sensible if it is. A professional adviser should be consulted in this respect. Under Scottish law, the declaration of trust is required to be in writing in any event.

CHAPTER 4

Shareholders' Agreements ***

The balance of power under company law

This book contains many examples of two balances of power under company law. The first is the balance between the freedom of the directors to manage the business of the company profitably, and the need to prevent them from abusing that freedom. The second is the balance to be struck as to the respective powers and rights of the shareholders as against each other.

The Companies Acts and the courts establish a framework within which these two balances are set. It assumes that, subject to certain safeguards against abuse, majority shareholders should have their way.

However, companies are often owned and managed by two or more people who see themselves as having a relationship more akin to a partnership than the relationship envisaged between shareholders under company law – a relationship often referred to as a 'quasi-partnership' by lawyers.

Alternatively, the company may be wrapped around a family hierarchy, or there may be outside investors, or employee shareholders. In all of these instances, there may be good reasons why the usual framework is inappropriate.

Using the articles

Provided sufficient shareholders agree, the articles may be used to vary the framework. The shareholders have the option of either relaxing their usual control over the affairs of their company or, more commonly, of tightening the screw, by provision in the articles.

However, two particular problems arise. The first is that the courts will generally only recognise the articles as being capable of giving rights to any shareholder in his capacity as a shareholder. If the articles confer any other rights, they will not be enforceable either by or against the company. The second is that the courts will not always allow one shareholder to enforce a right given to him by the articles directly against another shareholder.

Shareholders' agreements as a solution

As a result of these problems, the use of shareholders' agreements is common. The shareholders' agreement is a contract entered into between shareholders of a company to regulate the manner in which their company is to be run, and certain aspects of their relationship with each other. Commonly, shareholders who wish to deviate from the general principle of majority rule will use both special articles, and also a shareholders' agreement to achieve their aim. The provisions of each will supplement the other and the two will operate in tandem so as to meet the wishes of the shareholders. Provisions which might not be enforceable if included in one are included in the other. By this means, shareholders can achieve virtually any balance of power that they wish.

The nature of a shareholders' agreement

Usually, the shareholders' agreement operates as a private voting agreement as to how the shareholders will behave in relation to the company. The shareholders can agree amongst themselves, for example, that they will only vote to alter the articles if they all agree, and this will be enforceable between them. The company itself will often also be a party to the agreement, although there are technical rules which usually mean that the company should only agree to be bound by some, and not all, of the provisions of the agreement.

This is because of certain complicated case-law regulating the extent to which the directors of a company can agree something now which will fetter the company's ability to do certain things in the future. This case-law means that professional advice on the agreement is even more important if the company is a party to it.

So, first, what are the features of a shareholders' agreement as against articles of association, and, secondly, which matters are commonly and appropriately dealt with in a shareholders' agreement?

Features of a shareholders' agreement

(1) Shareholders' agreements can confer personal rights on the parties to the agreement, whilst articles generally cannot.
(2) Shareholders' agreements create a direct right of action by any one party to the agreement against any other.
(3) Shareholders' agreements, if properly drafted, remain confidential.
(4) Shareholders' agreements cannot be altered except with the consent of every party to them.
(5) For a new shareholder to be bound by the shareholders' agreement, he must specifically agree to become a party to it.

As a result of this, a rule of thumb which is often applied when comparing the benefits of including a provision in articles rather than an agreement, or vice versa, is to ask whether the provisions being introduced are relevant only to the particular shareholders of the company at the time, or are intended to apply also to all persons who might become shareholders in the future. If the former, an agreement is more appropriate. If the latter, the articles are more appropriate.

(6) The remedies available to a shareholder on breach of the agreement may differ from those available on breach of an identical provision in the articles.

Matters commonly found in shareholders' agreements

The contents of a shareholders' agreement will depend upon the relationship envisaged between the shareholders of that company, but the following checklist will look familiar to an adviser who is used to dealing with agreements of this type.

– Can the power of the minority shareholder to participate in management be protected? The agreement may give the minority shareholder the right to require appointment of himself, or a person nominated by him, as a director, even though his holding would not usually be sufficient to enable him to do this.

– Will the minority holder receive sufficient information as to the company's affairs? It is common to require that certain management accounts and documents are made available to the minority shareholder to which he would not normally be entitled.

– Could the majority shareholder force through changes which the minority holder considers crucial to his interests? A minority shareholder is frequently given the power to veto certain decisions, which he would normally have little or no power to influence.

– Are there positive obligations which the minority shareholder wishes to be able to enforce, such as for the company to declare a dividend whenever it can?

– Can the minority shareholder 'escape' if he wishes? The agreement invariably deals with the circumstances in which a shareholder may sell his shares and it is always crucial to ensure that any formula for valuing the shares is both fair and fully understood by the parties. If, as is common, the agreement provides for remaining parties to the agreement to acquire the shares of any party who dies, the agreement will usually require each party to take out life cover, in favour of the others, so that they have funds to pay for the shares.

The possible methods of regulating how shareholders deal with their shares are virtually infinite. However, the comments on the possible contents of articles of association in relation to transfer at pp 47 et seq are also relevant in this context.

Conclusion

Shareholders' agreements offer enormous scope for tailoring legal rights and liabilities to the needs of a particular company and its shareholders. They should, however, be approached with caution – the amateur shareholders' agreement should be avoided, since, if it is ever relied upon, it is more likely to benefit litigation lawyers than the parties to it. Care must also be exercised in relation to the tax consequences of entering into a shareholders' agreement, both in relation to the shareholders' own position, and in relation to the company concerned. In every respect, professional advice is essential.

CHAPTER 5

Directors and Other Officers

Officers

The officers of a company are usually the directors and the secretary. For some purposes, an auditor is treated as an officer, in the sense that he has a duty to the company when carrying out certain activities. There may be other officers, but these are unusual.

There is no definition of a director or secretary in the Companies Acts. However, the Companies Acts do say that the word director 'includes any person occupying the position of a director, by whatever name called'. This means someone may be a director who has not been given that title. For example, directors of a company may be called the council of management, but they are still its directors, and subject to all the rules which apply to directors. A company may be the director or secretary of another company. So may a Scottish partnership or a Limited Liability Partnership, since these are legal entities. However, the same is not true of an ordinary English or Northern Irish partnership.

Directors' duties **

Despite the fact that there is no definition of a director in the Companies Acts, it is possible to provide a rough definition of a director by reference to his duties, as discussed from time to time in the courts. Whilst this produces only general principles it is nevertheless correct to say that a director is a person appointed by the shareholders to manage the business of the company. This means that the job of director will vary from company to company. A director of a major company will be managing a very different business from a director of a very small company. The way in which a director manages the business of the company will also vary according to whether he is one of a number of directors forming a board of directors, or whether he is a sole director.

Secretary's duties

The job of the secretary is easier to define. He is responsible for compliance with those provisions of the Companies Acts which require the company to keep registers, and make its affairs open to the public, and he is also recognised by the courts as the chief administrative officer of the company. The secretary's responsibility for compliance with the provisions of the Companies Acts in respect of registers and publicity is shared with the directors.

The secretary may also have additional responsibilities under his contract of employment, but these are not statutory responsibilities and will vary widely from company to company.

Controlling the directors **

In managing the business of the company, the directors are in an extremely powerful position. They look after the affairs of the company, and are in a position of trust. They might abuse their position in order to profit at the expense of their company, and therefore at the expense of the shareholders of the company.

Consequently, the law imposes a number of duties, burdens and responsibilities upon directors, to prevent abuse. Much of company law can be seen as a balance between allowing directors the freedom to manage the company's business so as to make a profit, and preventing them from abusing this freedom.

The Companies Acts

The directors of the company are unable to make certain important decisions. The Companies Acts provide that some decisions must be made by, or with the specific authority of, the shareholders. These are set out in Chapter 15.

The memorandum of association

When managing the business of the company, the directors must only carry on activities which are authorised by the company's objects and powers set out in, or implied as a result of the wording of, the company's memorandum. The Companies Acts provide that it is the shareholders who decide the company's objects and powers. If the directors want the company to carry on a business not authorised by the shareholders, they must call upon the shareholders to alter the memorandum.

The articles of association

When managing the business of the company, the directors must act in accordance with the company's articles of association. The contents of the articles are a matter for decision by the shareholders. The shareholders may have included restrictions on the directors in the articles. For example, it was once common to find a provision in articles which said that the directors could borrow money from a lender on behalf of their company, but only up to a certain amount. If the borrowing exceeded a specified figure (usually a sum equivalent to the company's issued share capital) the directors had to seek the consent of the shareholders. Such a provision is rare in modern articles, but it illustrates the type of control which may be exercised by the shareholders if they wish.

A more common provision to be found in modern articles is a direction as to the manner in which directors must exercise their powers to allot new shares. Ordinarily, modern articles provide that, when allotting new shares, directors must offer new shares to the existing shareholders, in proportion to their shareholdings, unless the shareholders waive this requirement by special resolution. This is important to a majority share-holder, who wants to retain control of a company in the event that new shares are issued.

The articles will also contain rules as to how directors meet to make decisions, how they delegate their authority, and how they exercise their powers.

Articles sometimes require a proportion of the directors to retire at the annual general meeting and seek re-election by the shareholders if they wish to continue in office. This is called 'retirement by rotation' and is a classic example of control over directors – a periodic review of their position as directors. However, most modern articles do not require directors to retire by rotation.

Disclosure requirements

Directors are required by the Companies Acts to reveal to the board the nature of their interest or involvement in any agreements, transactions or arrangements entered into by their company, whether a direct or indirect interest or involvement. The disclosure must be to the full board – disclosure to a committee of the directors is not sufficient. There is case-law that suggests that such disclosure must be made and minuted even when the company has a sole director, so he is declaring the nature of his interest or involvement to himself!

Particularly, a director is required to notify the company of his interests in its shares, or shares of other companies in the same group. For example, he may own such shares, or an option to buy them.

Often the directors are also required to reveal interests of people connected with them – the interests of such people are treated as theirs. Such 'connected people' include the director's spouse and the director's children who are under 18.

It is good practice for the chair to remind directors of their various obligations as to disclosure at the beginning of every board meeting, to prompt their compliance, if appropriate.

In certain circumstances, a transaction involving a director must be approved by the shareholders before it may be entered into by the company. These circumstances are included in the list of matters requiring a decision of the shareholders in Chapter 15.

Disqualification and wrongful trading

The law on insolvency allows directors to be disqualified from being directors of any company if they have acted improperly. In some circumstances, a director can be required to help pay the debts of his company, even though it is a separate legal person. For example, directors of a company who try to 'trade out of difficulty' and fail may be found guilty of 'wrongful trading' and can be made personally liable.

General duties arising from legal decisions in the courts

There are a number of cases in which the courts have evolved guidelines as to how directors must act. These may be summarised in a number of ways.

(1) The directors must always exercise their powers for a 'proper purpose' that is, in furtherance of the reason for which they were given those powers by the shareholders. For example, directors are given power to issue shares in order to raise money for the company. If shares are issued for another purpose, such as to increase the number of shares held by a particular director, the board may be found to have acted other than for a proper purpose. Directors are particularly vulnerable if they have acted in a way which benefits themselves.

(2) Directors must act in good faith in what they honestly believe to be the best interests of the company, and not for any collateral purpose. This means that, particularly in the event of a conflict between the company's interests and their own, the directors must always favour the company.

(3) Directors must act with due skill and care. Whilst the courts will recognise that a director may make mistakes, or even act stupidly, there is a bottom line – a minimum duty of skill and care – below which a director must not fall. Increasingly, the courts have started saying that a director with special knowledge or skills – perhaps financial skills gained through accountancy qualifications – must apply that knowledge or those skills when acting as a director. The minimum duty of skill or care expected of directors with special skills is therefore higher than the norm.

(4) Directors must consider the interests of employees of the company.

Shadow directors *

In many circumstances, the law applies not only to a director, but to a 'shadow director'. A shadow director is a person in accordance with whose directions or instructions the directors of a company are accustomed to act. Under this definition, it is possible that a director, or the whole board, of a holding company, and the holding company itself, could be treated as a shadow director of a subsidiary. Judicial comments in legal cases suggest that a bank manager could also be treated as a shadow director of a company if he intervenes in its affairs but that this would only occur if circumstances were exceptional. The problem of shadow directorships can become more acute when a company is approaching insolvency, or has become insolvent.

Professional advisers giving advice in their professional capacity are specifically excluded from the definition of a shadow director in the companies legislation.

Directors and employees **

Care should be taken to distinguish between the status of a director and of an employee. A director is not necessarily also an employee, although he may be. This can be important for the purposes of unfair dismissal and redundancy law. Very simply, a director will also be an employee for these purposes if he has a service contract with the company.

Sole directors **

A private company may, if its articles allow, have only one director, provided that the sole director is not the secretary as well. One company may be a director of another and this is common in groups of companies. For example, company 'B' may be a director of company 'A'. However, if it is the sole director of company 'A' and it has only one director itself, that person may not also be the secretary of company 'A'. A public company must have two directors.

Consequently (assuming A and B are private companies), the following examples illustrate various situations as either permitted or not permitted.

Appointment of a director *

Upon issue of the certificate of incorporation of a company, a person who has consented to act as a director when the application for incorporation is made is automatically constituted a director of the company – no appointment or confirmation of his appointment is required.

Subject to the disqualifications and restrictions in the Companies Acts as to who may be a director, the method of appointment of subsequent directors is laid down in the company's articles. The ultimate control as to the composition of the board of directors rests with the shareholders who can always appoint, and – more importantly sometimes – dismiss a director. The shareholders can also fix the minimum and maximum number of directors. However, the board can usually appoint (but not dismiss) a director to his office as well.

Before appointing a director, both the shareholders and the board should check a number of procedural matters, in addition to assessing the competence of the prospective director.

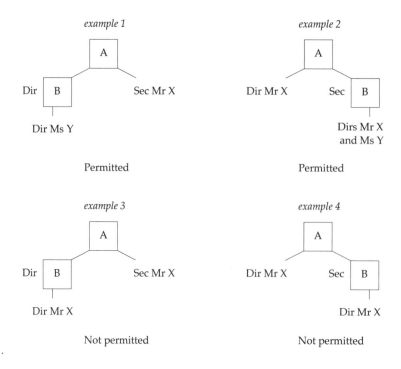

Figure 8 – Examples of sole directors and non-sole directors

The articles should be checked for any nationality or other restriction on directors. The permitted maximum number of directors should also be checked although there may be no maximum number. If there is, it will have been fixed by the shareholders. If the maximum number needs increasing before a new director may be appointed, the directors will need to ask the shareholders to increase it.

Sometimes directors are required by the articles to also hold shares. This is called a 'share qualification'. The articles will specify the number of shares required to be held. If a share qualification is required, the director must acquire sufficient shares within 2 months of his appointment or such earlier time as is prescribed by the articles. Share qualifications are now relatively rare.

If letterheads and other business stationery include details of directors, these should be amended by the addition of the new director's details. Letterheads must include details of either all, or none, of the directors.

The company's bankers should be advised of the appointment. The board may need to alter the instructions as to signatories to the company's bank account if the director is to be authorised to operate the company's bank account.

The company must always obtain the proposed director's particulars and consent to act on the official form. Alternatively, if the appointment is to be notified to Companies House electronically, the director must provide three items of personal information from a list of nine. These items are included in the electronic notification to Companies House as evidence of the director's consent to act.

The form or electronic notification must be lodged at Companies House within 14 days of the date of appointment. There is no fee.

A similar form or electronic notification must also be lodged if the director's particulars alter, within 14 days of the date of the alteration.

Once the new director has been appointed, the secretary must amend the register of directors and perhaps the register of directors' interests in shares.

Vacation of office **

Unless the director's continuation in office, or appointment, is sanctioned by the shareholders, either at a general meeting or in the articles, a director of a public company or a private company which is the subsidiary of a public company must either vacate office at the conclusion of the annual general meeting next following the date on which he attains the age of 70, or may not be appointed director of such a company.

If the company is a public company or a subsidiary of a public company, seek legal advice in this respect. However, directors of a private company are not usually subject to any age limit.

Bankruptcy is usually also a ground for vacation of office under the articles. In addition, it is a criminal offence for an undischarged bankrupt to act as director or liquidator of, or directly or indirectly to take part in or be concerned in the promotion, formation or management of, any company except with the leave of the court by which he has been adjudged bankrupt.

A director may always be dismissed from office as a director by a majority vote of the shareholders, provided that a special procedure is followed. The procedure is complex, and legal advice will always be required.

Of course, a director who is removed from office may have rights in respect of his contract of employment. Legal advice should always be taken as to the rights of a director both before he is appointed and in the event of a proposed dismissal. Failure to do so could prove extremely expensive to the company.

In practice, the articles usually also provide for the following circumstances to give rise to vacation of office by a director:

(1) insanity or mental disorder;
(2) resignation;
(3) absence from meetings over a particular period;
(4) if there is one, failure to acquire a share qualification.

Within 14 days of any vacation of office, a form or electronic notification must be lodged notifying Companies House. There is no fee.

Resignation ***

A director may resign at any time, even if his fellow board members purport not to accept the resignation. The resignation need not be in writing but without a written resignation a director may find it difficult to prove whether he has resigned or, more commonly, precisely when he did so.

Resignation may constitute a breach of the director's contract of employment, if he is an employee of the company.

A form or electronic notification must be filed, within 14 days of the resignation, notifying Companies House. There is no fee. Technically, the form should be signed by an existing officer of the company. However, the registrar will accept a form signed by the resigned director even though, technically, he is no longer an officer.

Remuneration of directors *

Directors do not have any right to receive remuneration from the company simply because they are directors. A director who wants to keep the remuneration given to him, or in the case of a sole director, that he has given to himself, must be able to show some authority for that payment.

This authority usually appears in the articles – which will say that the shareholders determine the remuneration of the directors. In practice, the shareholders usually exercise this power by delegating it to the directors, who determine their own remuneration. The directors will always have in mind that, if they pay themselves too much, it is possible that they will be dismissed by the shareholders or find themselves defending court proceedings alleging their excessive remuneration is unfairly prejudicial to the shareholders, who would otherwise expect to receive a larger dividend.

The secretary

The company must have a secretary. If the company is a public company there are special rules as to who may act as secretary. Only a person with a professional qualification, or who is sufficiently experienced, may act as secretary of a public company. Any company may have a corporate secretary. There may be joint secretaries, or an assistant or deputy secretary. This can be useful, if the company secretary is not always available – for example, to sign the annual return.

The secretary is appointed, and may be removed, by resolution of the board of directors.

Service contracts ***

Ordinarily, a director or secretary will have a written service contract with the company which will define, amongst other things, his executive duties as an employee of the company, and the way in which his remuneration is calculated.

Legal advice will be required on the service agreement, in view of the employment legislation, the possible requirement to obtain approval of the shareholders to the agreement, and the requirements as to disclosure of its contents to the shareholders.

The contract will commonly deal not only with matters such as pay, and holidays, but will also restrict competition from the employee following a resignation, allow the company the right to own patents and inventions created by the director in the course of employment, etc.

Some contracts will have to be approved by the shareholders – primarily, those which will, or may, continue for more than 5 years – and there are special procedural rules as to how such approval must be given.

Almost all directors' service contracts must be kept at one of certain specified places, such as the registered office, and be open for inspection by shareholders, both daily and at the annual general meetings.

Directors' and officers' liability insurance ***

It is possible for companies to indemnify their directors, or to pay for and maintain insurance cover, to provide protection for directors against certain risks attached to their office. This insurance cover is known as Directors' and Officers' Liability Insurance ('D & O' insurance) and is increasingly common.

Both the extent of the risk which can be covered, and the tax treatment of premiums and payments, are under constant review, and the trend is towards making D & O insurance more attractive to companies and their directors.

The complexity of the rules, and the fact that they are a 'moving feast' means that professional advice is always required if D & O insurance is to be taken out.

CHAPTER 6

Directors' Meetings

Business at directors' meetings

Board meetings (ie meetings of the directors) are necessary to deal with matters of general policy and with other business which must be transacted in a more formal way. Other matters may usually be dealt with by committees of directors, or officers with a particular executive function, on a day-to-day basis. The conduct of board meetings is governed largely by the company's articles. Articles usually empower directors to meet together for the dispatch of business and to conduct the meetings as they see fit.

Calling a directors' meeting

When, and how often, board meetings are to be held will depend upon the company and the requirements of its business. In a private company, meetings will be held as and when there is business requiring the board's attention.

However, many companies have a procedure whereby it has been agreed by the directors that board meetings be held regularly at a fixed date and time, which all the directors know about. Consequently, directors' meetings may usually be called as informally or formally as the directors may decide amongst themselves. This is subject to any special procedure in the company's articles. Calling a meeting is sometimes called 'convening' a meeting.

Unless there is something unusual in the articles, the following procedure will apply.

(1) A director, or the secretary at the request of a director, may call a directors' meeting. A secretary may not call a meeting unless requested to do so by a director or the directors.

(2) A board meeting may be held anywhere in the world, provided that, given directors' ability to attend, the venue is reasonable. However, the place which a board meeting is held may affect its tax status so that meetings of a UK company should only be held outside the UK if appropriate advice has been taken.

(3) In the absence of a standard procedure, agreed by the directors, as to frequency and notice of board meetings each director must be given reasonable notice of the meeting, stating its date, time and place.

Commonly, 7 days' notice is given, but what is 'reasonable' depends in the last resort upon the circumstances. Even where it has become the practice to give a certain period of notice, it will often be permissible to give a shorter notice (eg because of very urgent business); but pressure to give shorter notice must sometimes be resisted if an ulterior motive is suspected, such as a desire to prevent a particular director from attending.

(4)   Notice should be given to each director, and even to a director who has indicated that he will not attend a meeting. Usually, articles allow notice to be dispensed with in the case of a director who is not in the UK when the notice is given. The shareholders should be asked to consider whether they wish to alter the articles if all or some of the directors are likely to be outside the UK when board meetings are called. If a director has appointed an alternate, the alternate should be given the same notice as the other directors. Notice should also be given to any person who is to attend for all or part of the meeting and any other person who may have to prepare a statement or provide information for the meeting.

(5)   Since a board meeting may deal with any of the company's affairs which require attention and which lie within the board's competence, there is no need for the notice to specify particular or special business unless the articles require this; routine business will often be described simply as 'general'. Nevertheless, it is good practice to see that notice, even of a routine meeting, contains at least a general indication of the business, with a more precise indication of anything out of the ordinary. The test that the courts have laid down is that the notice must contain sufficient information to enable a director to exercise his judgment as to whether to attend. In practice, a director should always use his utmost endeavours to attend board meetings.

(6)   Unless the articles specifically prohibit this, and provided the directors who receive notice in this way have expressly agreed to it, there is no reason why notice of a directors' meeting could not be faxed or emailed.

It would be prudent for the company to establish written rules governing the giving of notice of board meetings by these electronic means. These would deal with, for example, the circumstances in which an email is deemed received by a director. Professional advice is recommended if these means of giving notice are to be used – the law in this area is fast moving.

Most articles would permit notice to be given orally, either face to face or by phone, but it would be unwise to adopt this as a general practice.

Quorum

If there is not a quorum at a meeting, it may not take place. Articles usually allow the directors to fix the quorum necessary to transact their business. If they do not, the quorum is two. Alternatively, the articles may make other provisions for a quorum, and may even provide for one director to exercise all powers of a meeting of the directors. If the company has a sole director, this power is vital.

A quorum, however fixed, means a quorum competent to transact the particular business. Under most companies' articles, a director may not be counted in the quorum in relation to a resolution on which he is not entitled to vote. A quorum must be maintained throughout the business of the meeting unless the articles provide otherwise. The secretary should take care to obtain the signature of each director who is present, in the attendance book, if one is kept, and should ensure that a quorum of directors competent to vote is maintained at all times.

Alternate directors *

Modern articles will allow a director to appoint another director or any other person approved by the rest of the board, to act on his behalf as an unremunerated substitute, or 'alternate' director. This is useful if the director is abroad, though the power is not limited to this situation. The appointing director may also revoke the appointment. Both appointment and removal of an alternate should be in writing, and signed by the appointing director. The alternate is deemed to be a director 'for all purposes', unless the articles say otherwise, and counts towards the quorum unless the appointing director is also present at the meeting.

Articles may not permit the appointment of alternates at all, so articles should always be checked if an alternate is to be appointed.

The chairman of the board *

The articles usually provide for the election of a chairman of the board. They empower the directors to appoint one of their own number as chairman and to determine the period for which he is to hold office. If no chairman is elected, or the elected chairman is not present within 5 minutes of the time fixed for the meeting or is unwilling to preside, those directors in attendance may usually elect one of their number as chairman of the meeting.

The chairman will usually have a second or casting vote in the case of equality of votes. Unless the articles confer such a vote upon him, however, a chairman has no casting vote merely by virtue of his office. He will also have a number of other procedural powers such as the power to adjourn the meeting.

Since the chairman's position is of great importance, it is vital that his election is clearly in accordance with any special procedure laid down by the articles and that it is unambiguously minuted; this is especially important to avoid disputes as to his period of office. Care should also be taken to keep a clear record of his resignation or removal from office. Usually there is no special procedure for resignation. As for removal, articles usually empower the board to remove the chairman from office at any time. Proper and clear minutes are important in order to avoid disputes.

A common problem in disputes as to who is chairman (and therefore entitled to a casting vote) is that different directors have signed, say, a bank mandate form and a copy shareholder resolution, and both have purported to do so as chair without protest from other directors or the secretary. Directors and the secretary should monitor documents signed to ensure that this does not happen.

Procedural requirements at the meetings

The conduct of the meeting will usually be informal, subject to the overall control of the chairman, and any special rules set out in the articles. Strict rules of debate will usually be inappropriate.

Whilst there may be conventions as to the order of business in a particular company, these are merely rules of practice and not binding. The articles themselves will not usually deal with matters like the order of business, notice of motions, questions, etc.

Ideally, the result of discussion will be unanimity. A division of opinion which cannot be resolved must, however, be put to a vote. Subject to the articles, each director has a single vote and business is transacted by a majority of votes. If there is a tie, the chairman usually has a casting vote. The articles should be checked to see who can vote – sometimes a director is prohibited from voting on a matter in which he has an interest, either himself, or through his family, or his other business associates. However, a director's shareholding, or any other interest in the company's shares, will not usually stop him from voting.

Adjournment

Articles usually empower directors to regulate their proceedings as they see fit. This means that the power to adjourn is vested in the meeting as a whole unless expressly placed elsewhere (eg in the chairman), by the articles. Usually the articles allow both the meeting and the chairman to adjourn. Subject therefore to a contrary provision in the articles a motion (or informal suggestion) for adjournment may be put forward at any time and takes priority over the business then in hand. As a matter of practice, notice of the adjourned meeting should be sent to each director.

Signed resolutions in lieu of meeting

Articles invariably provide that a resolution in writing, signed by all the directors for the time being entitled to receive notice of board meetings, is as effective as a resolution passed at a duly convened meeting. This is an exceptional provision to be used only when a genuine need arises. For example, because there is sudden and urgent business and the directors cannot be summoned to a meeting at short notice, or the matter to be decided does not require any discussion at all. The resolution is only effective if signed by all directors entitled to notice.

Where an alternate has been appointed, the signature of either the alternate or the appointor will be sufficient.

Holding directors' meetings electronically

It is increasingly common for directors' meetings to be held electronically. However, a number of practical issues need to be resolved if this is not to cause problems. It is sensible for decisions on these issues to be included in the company's articles of association. Table A makes no provision for electronic meetings but modern articles of association will do so.

The articles should define the conditions necessary to hold a valid electronic meeting. The overriding requirement will usually be that the means of electronic communication enables each director to hear and be heard by the other participants. This means there can be a debate or exchange leading to a resolution in the best interests of the company, as there would be at a conventional meeting. Electronic board meetings commonly take the form of a telephone or videoconferencing link.

An important issue is to decide where the electronic board meeting is being held. In a conventional meeting, all the directors are gathered in one place. The meeting is clearly held in that place. However, if directors communicating electronically are in different places, where is the meeting held?

This could cause tax problems if, for example, a director or, more likely, a majority of the directors regularly participate in electronic board meetings from a jurisdiction which taxes companies, wherever incorporated, whose central management and control is located there. If the fiscal authorities learn that directors on their territory participate electronically in board meetings of a UK company, they may investigate further.

Where central management and control is exercised will be a question of fact under the law of the jurisdiction concerned. However, the articles of association may be persuasive under that law. It may, therefore, be important that they prescribe where the company considers the meeting is being held, or the basis upon which that question should be resolved so the local tax authority can be referred to them. For example, it is common for articles to say the meeting is deemed held where the chair is physically present or, alternatively, where the directors agree.

Records and minutes

Articles usually provide that the attendance list should be prepared for signature by each director who attends the meeting. Copies of the memorandum, articles, latest reports and accounts and other important company documents should be made available in case they are required at the meeting.

At the meeting the secretary should report any apologies for absence and record subsequent arrivals and departures; these matters should be minuted.

After the meeting draft minutes should be prepared from notes taken at the meeting. The purpose of these minutes is usually to record what was decided and not to report what was said. The secretary must not allow the minutes in these circumstances to become a report of what directors, especially dissenting directors, actually said; but, upon request, a director may be recorded as having dissented from a decision or voted against a resolution passed by a majority.

However, this usual rule may be displaced in the case of very important decisions, or by a company in financial difficulties. In such instances, the chair or the board as a whole, may wish to instruct the secretary to record in the minutes the reasons for certain decisions, or the basis upon which they were made. The minutes can then be produced if the decisions need to be justified at a later date, for example to prove to a subsequent liquidator that the directors have acted properly and, particularly, are not guilty of wrongful trading (see Chapter 12). Similarly, the secretary may be instructed to record reasons for dissent.

Minutes may be kept in a bound book but, in practice, are almost invariably kept in a loose-leaf book. This is permitted by the Companies Acts, subject to 'suitable precautions' being taken, such as numbering of the pages to prevent alteration. However, minutes of board and committee meetings do not have to be made available at the company's offices for inspection by members, unlike minutes of general meetings. They are usually, therefore, kept separately.

Any signed resolution in lieu of a meeting must be entered in the minute book.

Committees and executive officers

Directors are frequently authorised by articles to delegate some or all of their powers to a committee of members of the board (and such a committee may consist of a single director). The board may also authorise delegation to a managing or other executive director. A managing director is usually given the same powers as the rest of the board put together, so appointment of a managing director should not be made without very careful thought. See Chapter 8 in this respect. In any event, such delegation is revocable and may be made conditional. Accordingly, a committee may be set up ad hoc, or as a permanent institution, for example to execute documents or approve share transfers. In delegating functions the directors may prescribe the committee's procedures as well as its powers; for instance, as to voting and the appointment of a chairman. However, in default, the same rules apply to committees as to the main board.

It is vital for the main board to be sure that they have a proper system of supervision in respect of a committee or executive officer, since otherwise they are in breach of their duty to act in the best interests of the company. Such supervision might include a written specification of the powers of the committee or executive officer and/or a regular requirement to report back to the main board.

The minutes should be signed by the chair of the meeting, or of the next succeeding meeting, since they are not otherwise evidence of the proceedings at the meeting. The minutes are not required to be approved by the board as a whole but it is good practice if they are, especially if the chair of the next meeting was not present at the meeting to which the minutes relate.

CHAPTER 7

Shareholders' Meetings (General Meetings)

Extraordinary general meetings

An extraordinary general meeting is any meeting of the shareholders of the company other than the annual general meeting. An extraordinary general meeting will be called to deal with specific matters arising which require a decision of the shareholders, whereas the annual general meeting is a meeting of shareholders held once a year in any event.

Matters required to be referred to shareholders

The matters which require a decision of the shareholders will vary from company to company. Some matters must be referred to them in every company, such as a decision to increase the company's authorised share capital, because the Companies Acts require it. Other decisions may have to be referred to the shareholders of a particular company as a result of specific provision to that effect in the company's articles. The officers of the company need to be aware of the matters which must be referred to their shareholders.

The matters required to be referred to shareholders under the Companies Acts are set out in Chapter 15 or (in the case of elective resolutions of the shareholders) referred to later in this chapter.

Types of shareholders' resolution

Once the company's officers have identified a matter as one required to be referred to the shareholders, they must identify the type of decision or 'resolution' required to be made or 'passed' by its shareholders.

There are four types of decision or resolution, each of which has differing requirements as to the notice period required to be given of the shareholders' meeting at which it is to be considered, and as to the majority required if it is to be passed. The notice periods and majorities required reflect the different importance attached to each type of decision by the companies legislation and/or the company's articles.

The types of resolution can be summarised as follows.

Type of resolution	Notice period	Majority required	Requirements for filing with the registrar of companies
Ordinary resolution	14 clear days	Over 50% of the votes cast at the meeting	Not normally required to be filed, except for an increase in authorised share capital, shareholders' authority to the directors to allot shares, or to revoke an elective resolution
Special resolution	21 clear days	At least 75% of the votes cast at the meeting	*All* special resolutions must be filed
Extraordinary resolution	14 clear days	At least 75% of the votes cast at the meeting	*All* extraordinary resolutions must be filed
Elective resolution	21 clear days	100% of the votes of the shareholders	*All* elective resolutions must be filed

Calling an extraordinary general meeting

If the articles do not provide otherwise, the board may call extraordinary general meetings at any time. Calling a general meeting is often called 'convening' the meeting. If there are not sufficient directors present in the UK to have a board meeting, any director or any shareholder may call an extraordinary general meeting. They do this, in each case, by instructing the secretary to call the meeting.

In addition, shareholders may always requisition an extraordinary general meeting by depositing a document called a 'requisition' at the registered office. Shareholders who deposit a requisition must represent one-tenth or more of the total voting rights of the company at the date of deposit, or it is not effective.

If the requisition is effective the directors must, within 21 days of the deposit of the requisition at the registered office, resolve to call a general meeting. If the directors fail to do so, the requisitionists may themselves instruct the secretary to call a general meeting as if they were the directors, and may recover any expenses they have incurred.

If the board calls the general meeting, a board meeting should be held to resolve to call the extraordinary general meeting. The directors should instruct the secretary to call the meeting by sending out notices. The secretary must be instructed by the board to call the meeting and cannot call the meeting himself.

The notice *

Notice of an extraordinary general meeting must be in writing and will normally set out the wording of the resolutions to be proposed in full (and must do so in the case of special, extraordinary and elective resolutions). The notice must contain a statement regarding the right of a shareholder to appoint a proxy.

Consequently, the secretary should prepare the notice to include:

(1) the date, time and place of the meeting;
(2) details of business to be transacted including ordinary, extraordinary, special and elective resolutions;
(3) a reminder of the right of a shareholder to appoint proxies.

Failure to observe these requirements may mean the notice is invalid and of no effect.

To whom should notice be given?

The notice should be given to the persons entitled to receive it under the articles of association. Usually these are shareholders who hold shares carrying the right to vote, personal representatives (if the shareholder has died), the directors and the auditors.

The way in which notice is given ('the method of service') is dependent on the articles. Articles usually provide that notice is to be served personally or by post to a shareholder's registered address – the address in the register of shareholders.

The Electronic Communications Act 2000 has made it possible to give notice of a shareholders' meeting electronically – for example, by fax, email or by posting it on a website specified for that purpose. The key requirement is that the shareholder must agree to the means of giving notice. If given by fax or email the shareholder must provide the company with a fax number or email address for the purpose. If the notice is posted on a website the shareholder must be notified, by a method agreed with him in advance, of the fact that the accounts have been published, which site they are on and how to find them on that site. The rules are complex and companies should not give electronic notice without advice. However, the Institute of Chartered Secretaries has issued a *Guide to Recommended Best Practice* in this area that provides an excellent indication of the issues involved. It can be ordered from www.icsa.org.uk.

How much notice should be given?

If posted, notice is deemed under modern articles to be given 48 hours after posting. If given electronically, a notice is deemed served 48 hours after despatch.

The length of notice for calling an extraordinary general meeting is 14 clear days unless a special or elective resolution is proposed, or a resolution to appoint a director, in which case 21 clear days' notice is required. The day the notice is given and the day of the meeting are not counted in calculating the notice period. This can be very important when the notice is given by post, because, under the current version of Table A (if it applies to the company), it is not deemed given until 48 hours after posting. In circumstances where the accounts are to be presented to the meeting, a copy of the accounts must be sent to each shareholder (whether entitled to receive notice of the meeting or not) and debenture holder, and to other persons entitled to receive notice of general meetings 21 clear days before the meeting.

Short notice

If it is agreed by a majority in number of the shareholders who have the right to attend and vote at a meeting to be called to consider an ordinary, special or extraordinary resolution, and who hold not less than a certain percentage in nominal value of the shares giving that right, the meeting may be held on less than the 14 or 21 clear days' notice. The required percentage will vary according to the company, but it is usually 95 per cent. However, if the company has passed an appropriate elective resolution the percentage required may be less. In any event, it cannot be reduced to less than 90 per cent (see Figure 9 at p 86). The rules as to short notice are different for extraordinary general meetings called to consider elective resolutions and for annual general meetings. These are considered later in this chapter.

If accounts are to be put before a meeting to be held at short notice, every shareholder should waive the right to receive them 21 days before the meeting.

Consent to short notice need not be given in writing, but it invariably is. The written consent should be kept with the company records.

What is the business of the meeting?

Matters dealt with at an extraordinary general meeting will be those specific matters for which the meeting is called. See Chapter 15 for some of the matters requiring a decision by ordinary, special or extraordinary resolution at a general meeting.

Signed resolutions in lieu of a meeting – written resolutions *

The Companies Acts permit shareholders of a private company to pass resolutions without holding an extraordinary general meeting, provided every shareholder entitled to vote at general meetings so wishes. However, this is not permitted in relation to the annual general meeting.

The resolution can instead be passed by every shareholder signing a resolution in writing – either the same document, or several documents each of which accurately states the terms of the resolution.

A written resolution can be used to pass every single sort of resolution including an elective resolution, and it is as good as if an extraordinary general meeting had been held, and all necessary formalities observed – the only exceptions are resolutions to remove a director, and to remove an auditor before the end of his period of office. However, some written resolutions are not effective unless and until a copy of them has been sent to the auditors, or they are otherwise notified of its contents, at or before the time the resolution is supplied to the shareholders for signature.

A copy of the resolution must be kept, and a record of the signatures on it, as if it were minutes of a meeting, and, if the resolution would have had to be lodged if passed at a general meeting, the written resolution must be lodged.

The annual general meeting of the shareholders *

A company must hold its first annual general meeting within 18 months of its incorporation. From then onwards it must hold an annual general meeting in every calendar year, and not more than 15 months must elapse between one annual general meeting and the next.

The annual general meeting gives the shareholders at least one opportunity every year to question the directors, and require them to account for the manner in which they have carried on the company's business.

However, where shareholders of a private company agree that they do not require such an opportunity, they may pass an elective resolution to dispense with the requirement to hold an annual general meeting. An elective resolution will have effect until revoked by an ordinary resolution.

If an elective resolution has been passed to dispense with the need to hold an annual general meeting any shareholder may, provided he does so before the end of September in any year, require an annual general meeting to be held in that year.

Calling the annual general meeting

Articles invariably authorise the board to call the annual general meeting at any time. If there are not sufficient directors present in the UK to hold a board meeting any director or any shareholder may call the annual general meeting. This is done, in either case, by asking the secretary to prepare and send out notices.

The notice

All notices of the annual general meeting must be in writing, and will set out the nature of the business to be conducted at the meeting. If this includes consideration of formal resolutions, the wording of these resolutions will normally be set out in full (and must be in the case of special, extraordinary or elective resolutions). The notice must contain a statement regarding the right of a shareholder to appoint a proxy.

The secretary should prepare the notice to include:

(1)   a statement that the meeting is the annual general meeting;
(2)   the date, time and place of the meeting;
(3)   details of business to be transacted including ordinary, extraordinary, special and elective resolutions;
(4)   a reminder of the right of a shareholder to appoint proxies.

Failure to observe these requirements means the notice is *invalid and of no effect.*

As with notice of extraordinary general meetings, notice can be given electronically (see p 81).

To whom should notice be given?

The notice should be given to the persons entitled to receive it under the articles of association. Usually these are shareholders who hold shares carrying the right to vote, personal representatives (if a shareholder has died), the directors, and the auditors.

The method of service is dependent on the articles. Articles usually provide that notice is to be served personally or by post to a shareholder's registered address – the address in the register of shareholders.

How much notice should be given?

If posted, notice is deemed under modern articles to be given 48 hours after posting. If given electronically, a notice is deemed given 48 hours after despatch.

The length of notice for calling an annual general meeting is always 21 clear days' notice. The day the notice is given and the day of the meeting are not counted in calculating the notice period. This can be very important when the notice is given by post, because it is not deemed given until 48 hours after posting. In circumstances where the accounts are to be presented to the meeting, a copy of the accounts must be sent to each shareholder (whether entitled to receive notice of meetings or not), and debenture holder, and to other persons entitled to receive notice of general meetings 21 clear days before the meeting.

Short notice

If *every* shareholder entitled to attend and vote at the annual general meeting consents to the meeting being called upon shorter notice than 21 clear days *and*, if accounts are to be put before the meeting, waives the right to receive them 21 days before the meeting, the meeting may be held on less than 21 clear days' notice.

This differs from the rules as to short notice for an extraordinary general meeting (see Figure 9).

Consent to short notice need not be given in writing, but it invariably is. The written consents should be kept with the company records.

What is the business of the meeting?

The usual matters dealt with at an annual general meeting are as follows.

Election of directors	If the company's articles require directors to retire by rotation at the annual general meeting those retiring at the annual general meeting will be considered for re-election (if they are offering themselves for re-election).
Accounts	Subject to any elective resolution dispensing with the requirement to put those documents before the shareholders in a general meeting, the profit and loss account and balance sheet together with the statutory reports on it may be laid before the meeting.
Dividend	If there is any dividend to be paid to shareholders on their shares the directors will propose it and the shareholders will vote to declare it.
Auditors	Subject to any elective resolution dispensing with the requirement to reappoint auditors annually, auditors are appointed to hold office from one general meeting at which accounts are laid to the next such general meeting. Therefore if accounts are being laid at the annual general meeting, and no such elective resolution has been passed, the reappointment of the auditors will be considered and their remuneration may be fixed (or the directors will be authorised to fix it at a later date).

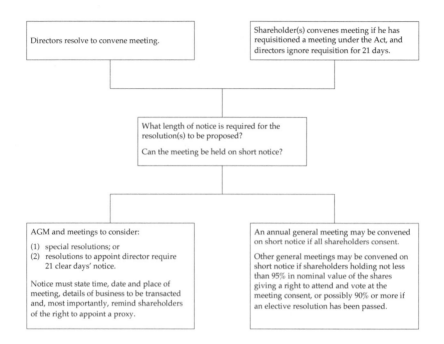

Figure 9 – Calling a general meeting

If a certain proportion of shareholders make a written requisition before the meeting, requiring additional business to be put before the shareholders at the annual general meeting, the annual general meeting must consider the resolution proposed by those shareholders. The requisitioning shareholders can also require a statement to be circulated before the meeting, by the company on their behalf, to those shareholders who are entitled to receive notice of the meeting.

Generally

Who is present?

The secretary should ascertain and list who is present, for the minutes. Provision of an attendance list for signature by all attendees is sensible from the secretary's point of view.

Quorum

A quorum must be present. Normally the required quorum is two persons entitled to vote on the business of the meeting. If a quorum is not present throughout the meeting, the meeting usually ceases to be effective. The articles should be carefully checked in these respects.

In the case of a private company, it may be a single member company. Such a company is permitted to hold either an extraordinary general meeting or the annual general meeting at which only the single shareholder is present, and the single shareholder will constitute a quorum at that meeting, irrespective of any provisions of law, or of the company's articles, to the contrary. However, it is prudent to alter the articles of a proposed single shareholder company in any event, so as to achieve consistency between the articles and the rules. The single shareholder must still be given formal notice of any general meeting and, if it is to be held on short notice, he must consent to the short notice as if he was one of a number of shareholders.

Otherwise, it is only in very exceptional circumstances that one person may constitute an effective meeting, or quorum, at a meeting. Subject to those circumstances, it is still not possible for one shareholder to constitute a meeting, or a quorum at it, where the company in fact has more than one shareholder, but the others choose not to attend at a proposed general meeting.

Chairman

The chairman of the board (if any) is usually also entitled to be chairman at shareholders' meetings if he is present and willing to act. If not, the directors nominate one of their number to act as chairman of the meeting. If no director is present and willing to act, the shareholders may choose one of their number to be chairman of the meeting.

Voting procedure

During the meeting, and subject to the articles, any resolution put to the vote will be decided on a show of hands unless before, or on the declaration of the result of the show of hands, a poll is demanded. The chairman, or two shareholders, or a single shareholder holding at least one-tenth of the issued shares has the right to demand a poll. On a poll, each shareholder normally has one vote for each share he holds. Ordinarily, only shareholders present in person, or corporations present by their representatives, may vote on a show of hands. Proxies may only vote on a poll, or a demand for a poll.

Records and registers *

After the conclusion of the meeting, minutes recording the proceedings and resolutions passed may be prepared, signed by the chairman and kept with the company's records.

Any requirements to file special resolutions or other items with the registrar of companies must be complied with.

The annual return *

Under the Companies Acts, every company must submit an annual return to Companies House every year, with a fee.

The annual return contains information as to the share capital, shareholders and officers of the company.

An annual return is sent to the company by Companies House each year, setting out the registrar of companies' understanding of the company's details. The secretary will check it, amend it if necessary and return it to Companies House, signed by him or a director. The annual return will be made up as at a date not later than the anniversary of formation of the company, or, if different, the anniversary of the last annual return date and must be lodged within 14 days of that date.

However, it is possible for the company to prepare and lodge its own annual return – for example if it wishes to alter the date to which it makes up its annual return in each year. The secretary should ask the auditor to deal with preparation of the annual return because there are complex rules as to the date to which the annual return should be made up and filed with the registrar of companies.

Proxies and representatives

Whether a shareholder is an individual or a company ('a corporate shareholder') and wishes to appoint someone to act for him at a general meeting of the shareholders, he may appoint a proxy. This applies to single shareholders of single member companies, as well as to any other shareholder of a company. The proxy may be able to vote at the meeting, but only on a poll, or a demand for a poll – he may not vote on a show of hands.

An appointment of a proxy must be in writing and be lodged at the company's registered office 48 hours before the meeting. The wording of a possible form of proxy is set out in Table A. There are two versions – either the shareholder may give his proxy a choice as to how he is to vote, or the shareholder may set out on the form the way he wishes the proxy to vote on particular resolutions.

If the company agrees, and provides an 'address' for the purpose, shareholders can send a form of proxy to the company electronically. 'Address' includes an email address or fax number. The rules are complex and companies should not offer shareholders the option of serving proxies electronically without advice. However, the Institute of Chartered Secretaries has issued a *Guide to Recommended Best Practice* in this area that provides an excellent indication of the issues involved. It can be ordered from www.icsa.org.uk.

Where a *corporate* shareholder wishes to appoint someone to act for it at a meeting, it can appoint either the proxy or a representative. The word 'representative' has a strict legal meaning in this context.

In practice, it is usually best for a corporate shareholder to appoint a representative, because a representative has power to speak, and vote not only on a poll or demand for a poll but also on a show of hands. Appointment of a representative also gets over the problem of having to lodge the form of proxy at the company's registered office 48 hours prior to the meeting – the representative merely needs to turn up at the meeting with a copy of an appropriate board resolution of the corporate shareholder, certified as a true copy by a director or the secretary of the corporate shareholder.

Elective resolutions *

There are certain matters which may be dispensed with by an elective resolution of the shareholders. These allow the shareholders to relax certain requirements of the Companies Acts which would otherwise apply to the company. Only private companies can pass elective resolutions.

The requirements which may be relaxed are as follows.

The requirement to hold an annual general meeting every year

A company can pass an elective resolution before 30 September in any year, dispensing with the need to hold an annual general meeting in that year, and any subsequent year, until the elective resolution is either revoked or ceases to have effect.

The requirement to lay the accounts before the shareholders at a general meeting of the shareholders

A company can pass an elective resolution allowing accounts to be sent to shareholders and the auditors, rather than laid before a general meeting of the shareholders. The elective resolution has effect for the financial year in which it is made, and every subsequent year, until the elective resolution is revoked or ceases to have effect. The accounts can be sent at any time not less than 28 days before the end of the period allowed for delivery of the accounts to the registrar of companies.

The accounts must be accompanied by a notice telling the shareholder of his right to require that a general meeting be held to consider the accounts.

Alternatively, provided a shareholder agrees, accounts can be sent to him electronically to an 'address' notified by him for the purpose. An address includes an email address or fax number. The accounts can also be posted on a website designed for the purpose. In the latter case the shareholder must be notified, by a method agreed with him in advance, of the fact that the accounts have been published, which site they are on and how to find them on that site. The rules are complex and companies should not send or post accounts electronically without advice. However, the Institute of Chartered Secretaries has issued a *Guide to Recommended Best*

Practice in this area that provides an excellent indication of the issues involved. It can be ordered from www.icsa.org.uk.

The requirement that auditors be re-elected annually

An elective resolution can be passed to dispense with the need to re-elect auditors annually. The auditors are otherwise required to retire at every general meeting at which the accounts are laid before the shareholders.

The auditors will then be deemed to be re-elected every year and stay in office either until a resolution is passed to exempt the company from the need to appoint auditors because it has become dormant, or until a resolution is passed to the effect that the auditors' appointment be brought to an end, so that they are not deemed reappointed or until an ordinary resolution is passed to revoke the elective resolution.

The requirement that shareholders give the directors an authority to allot shares which cannot exceed 5 years

An elective resolution can be passed to the effect that the shareholders can give the directors an authority to allot shares for any fixed period, or even for an indefinite period, rather than for the maximum period of 5 years which otherwise applies.

The shareholders of the company can then give such an authority by ordinary resolution, or in the articles, in any way envisaged by the elective resolution.

The requirement that extraordinary general meetings held on short notice be so held only if the holders of 95 per cent in nominal value of the shares agree

An elective resolution can be passed to reduce the percentage of shareholders' consent required to hold an extraordinary general meeting on short notice down to a minimum of 90 per cent.

Passing the elective resolution

An elective resolution is not effective unless it is passed at a general meeting at which all shareholders are present, in person or by proxy (or, in the case of a corporate shareholder, its representative), and all agree to the elective resolution being passed. Twenty-one clear days' notice must be given of the meeting and the notice must state the terms of the resolution and the fact that it is an elective resolution. However, if every shareholder entitled to attend and vote at the general meeting consents to the meeting being called upon shorter notice than 21 clear days, the meeting may be held on less than 21 clear days' notice. The elective resolution must be lodged with the registrar of companies within 15 days after it is passed.

An elective resolution may also be passed as a written resolution without the need to hold a general meeting, but this should not be attempted without professional advice.

Revocation or cessation of an elective resolution

An elective resolution can be revoked by an ordinary resolution – such an ordinary resolution must be lodged with the registrar of companies within 15 days after it is passed. It will also cease to have effect if the company ceases to be private, by re-registering as a public company.

CHAPTER 8

Contracts Binding on the Company

Types of contract

Individuals enter into contracts or agreements (the two words mean the same thing) every day – by making a purchase in a shop, buying a car park ticket or signing a contract of employment, for example. Most contracts need not be in writing. With a car park ticket some parts of the contract are written and some are not. Some contracts must be in writing.

The objects and powers of the company

Provided it is empowered to do so in its memorandum, a company can also enter into contracts. Again, these need not be in writing, unless the law requires it.

The company may not be empowered to enter into the contract, because of limits in its memorandum. A company which acts outside its memorandum is acting 'ultra vires' – beyond its powers.

Whilst 'outsiders' are not concerned as to whether the company is acting ultra vires or not, it remains the duty of the directors to ensure that it is not.

Decision by the board

Usually, a decision of the board of directors will bind the company. But it may be the case that the directors cannot bind the company to a particular transaction – there may be limits which the shareholders have put on them, in the memorandum or articles. However, a person dealing with the company in good faith is entitled to assume that the board, or any person authorised by the board, can bind the company. The directors of the company will get into trouble with the shareholders and the company, for exceeding their power to bind the company, but the company is still bound.

Decisions by single directors, secretaries or employees

The directors of a company rarely make a decision at a full board meeting, although they should do so where matters of policy are concerned, or other issues considered crucial to the operation of the company, or where a formal written record of particular decisions is required. Instead, it is often single directors, or the secretary, or other employees who enter into contracts with outsiders, on behalf of the company.

Can a person entering into an agreement with a single director, or the secretary, or an employee, of a company be sure that the company will be bound to observe the agreement?

Actual authority

It is open to the directors to delegate some of their authority to one or more of their number – to committees of directors. Some of the powers can even be delegated to one director who holds an executive office, such as finance director. Indeed, when a company appoints a managing director, he sometimes has all the powers of the rest of the board. An outsider dealing with a committee, or single director, or managing director, with actual authority to bind the company on a particular matter, is safe.

Similarly, the directors can delegate their powers to the secretary, or any employee. The signature on a document of an ordinary employee with actual authority to sign that document will bind the company – for example, a receptionist who has actual authority to sign for registered post can bind the company in that respect, in the same way as a director could.

The general principle is that any person with actual authority in a particular matter can bind the company.

From the company's point of view it is crucial that every director, secretary and employee knows the limits of his actual authority – it is vital to establish a chain of authority. Contracts of employment, staff regulations and standing orders, and job descriptions can all help set these limits.

Ostensible authority

What if an employee, for example, exceeds his actual authority? 'Holding out' – the principle of ostensible authority – may apply. This means that an outsider is entitled to assume the employee (or director or secretary) is able to bind the company because, for example, his title implies a certain status, or he has regularly entered into agreements of the same nature before, with the knowledge of the board of directors, but without objection from them.

Whenever an employee is given a special title such as manager, or divisional director, consideration should be given as to the effect this will have on outsiders. Has the employee been given an 'ostensible authority' which he did not previously have?

Usual authority

Outsiders who do not know otherwise are entitled to assume that an officer or employee, who usually has power to bind a company to a particular type of contract, in fact has such power, even if he actually does not. A classic example is the secretary. It is usual, as a matter of general commercial practice for the secretary to be able to enter into administrative contracts on behalf of the company, and a secretary will therefore have usual authority for these purposes.

Directors have a wide usual and ostensible authority – the company holds them out as having very wide powers. The secretary has usual and ostensible authority in relation to administrative matters. For example, a bank manager would not accept the secretary's signature on a loan agreement, but an agreement for the supply of typewriters for the office would be a different matter.

It is a matter of degree in every case whether a particular employee, director or secretary has ostensible or usual authority. Whilst the company can seek compensation from someone with ostensible authority who exceeds their actual authority, the company is bound, and seeking compensation may be a useless remedy.

No actual, ostensible or usual authority

What if an employee, director or secretary has no actual, ostensible or usual authority, but holds himself out as having authority, and the outsider deals with the employee, director or secretary? The company is not bound, but the employee, director or secretary may be liable to the outsider for damages for breach of warranty of authority.

Executing documents – the law in England and Wales and Northern Ireland **

Generally, whoever binds the company should always sign 'for and on behalf of XYZ Limited', otherwise they are personally vulnerable. For example, a director who signs or authorises the signature of a cheque which does not have the proper company name on it will be personally liable to meet the cheque, and also liable to a fine.

In this context, company name means just what it says. Abbreviations, such as 'Bros' instead of 'Brothers' are not allowed if it is the latter which appears on the certificate of incorporation (or certificate on change of name) of the company.

Similarly, failure to include the company name on business letters, notices, official publications, invoices, receipts, letter of credit, and other official documents means that officers may have committed an offence, and be liable to a fine.

Contracts in writing should be signed as follows:

SIGNED by . . . .
for and on behalf of XYZ Limited

What about the seal? Every company may have a seal. The seal is the signature of the company, and its imprint on a document usually has to be witnessed by signature of a director and the secretary or two directors. They are not signing the document themselves – the effect of their signatures is merely to witness the affixing of the seal. Documents under seal should be executed as follows:

THE COMMON SEAL of
the company was affixed
hereto in the presence of:

AFFIX
SEAL
HERE

. . . . Director
. . . . Director/Secretary

Before the Companies Act 1989, companies *had* to have a seal, but this is no longer the case.

If a company does not wish to have or to use a seal, there are new rules governing how documents should be executed. Which of the new rules applies will depend upon whether the document is intended to be executed as a Deed or not.

Documents not intended to be Deeds must be signed by either a director and the secretary, or two directors, and expressed to be executed by the company. Documents executed this way might be executed as follows:

This document is hereby executed by XYZ Limited.

. . . . Director
. . . . Director/Secretary

If a document is intended to be a Deed, it must be signed in the same way, but must make it clear on its face that it is intended to be a Deed. For example, it might be executed as follows:

This document is hereby executed, with the intention that it be a Deed, by XYZ Limited.

. . . . Director
. . . . Director/Secretary

If in doubt as to the execution of documents, seek professional advice.

Executing documents – the law in Scotland ***

A company, wherever it is registered, may need to enter into a contract which is governed by Scottish law. Advice should, if the circumstances warrant, be sought from a qualified Scottish professional, in relation to creating and enforcing such contracts. However, the rules as to the power of the company to contract, and the position of its board and employees of the company, are the same, irrespective of whether the company is registered in Scotland, or in England and Wales.

However, execution of a document under Scottish law is a complex matter, and advice should always be sought from a qualified Scottish professional. Scottish law will apply to such documents, irrespective of whether the company is registered in Scotland or in England and Wales.

The current situation is that Scots law requires certain contracts and other legal transactions to be in writing. In addition, certain documents are required to be formally authenticated. If certain formalities are observed in the execution of a document, the document is presumed accurate and to have been executed by the granter, so that the burden of proof falls on the person who wishes to rebut the presumption.

Arriving at the current situation has not been plain sailing. Scots law has been reformed by the Companies Act 1989, the Law Reform (Miscellaneous Provisions) (Scotland) Act 1990 and the Requirements of Writing (Scotland) Act 1995. The latter Act introduced substantive reforms.

These reforms provide that only those documents referred to in the Act are required to be in writing, unless writing is specifically required in relation to a document under some other legislation.

If the granter is a company, the document may be signed by a director, the secretary or a duly authorised signatory. There is no requirement for a witness or use of a company seal, if the company has one.

If the document is to be recorded in, for example, the Scottish property register, it must be formally authenticated. This means that it must either:

(1) bear to have been subscribed by a director, secretary or authorised signatory and bear to have been signed by a witness to that subscription, and include the witness's name and address; or

(2) bear to have been subscribed by two directors, a director and the secretary or by two duly authorised signatories, without witnesses.

CHAPTER 9

Accounts

The word 'accounts' is often heard when business matters are being discussed. Correctly used, it describes the set of figures prepared by a company at intervals which summarise the business results of that period. Another common description of these accounts is the term, financial statements.

'Accounts' is also used frequently, and rather misleadingly, to describe the books and records which are kept by the company as evidence of the company's transactions.

These are correctly referred to as accounting records. Accounts then are a summary of the results for a period whilst accounting records provide evidence of day-to-day events and transactions. The accounts of a company will be prepared from the information recorded in the accounting records.

The different types of accounts which exist are discussed later on in this chapter.

The public has a legal right to information on the financial standing of a company with which it deals. Every company must send its statutory accounts to be filed in Companies House and the public may inspect and take copies of these accounts. The public has no access, however, to a company's accounting records. Accounting records are essential to enable the preparation of the annual statutory accounts and form the basis of the information which the company's auditor will inspect during the course of his audit of the company's statutory accounts.

Every business needs to keep some form of record of the transactions which take place. Without this record, it would be impossible to know what had happened in the past, who owed the business money, or indeed how much the business owed to others or held in the bank account at any point in time.

The need to keep records not only provides the businessman with information to help him run the company more efficiently, but also protects the public who deal with that company, as it ensures that an accurate record of all the company's transactions is maintained.

The basic accounting system

Over the years, as business developed, standard methods of recording transactions, or 'keeping books' have emerged. The traditional technique now is to maintain a system of 'double entry' books.

The double entry bookkeeping system records every aspect of each transaction the company makes. For example, if a computer retailing company sells a computer, the following entries would be made in that company's books:

On the debit (left) side	On the credit (right) side
Reduction in the value of stock at the cost price to the company of the computer.	Increase in the retained profits representing the difference between cost and retail prices.
Increase in cash at the retail price of the computer.	

The debit (left) side of the equation records *assets*, ie property or cash owned by the company or owed to it. This includes trade debtors (people who owe the company money for goods or services it has supplied). The credit (right) side records *liabilities*, ie amounts which the company owes to some other person. This includes trade creditors (to whom the company owes money for goods and services supplied), loans (which the company owes to lenders) and share capital and profit (both of which the company owes to its shareholders).

Setting up an accounting system

The accounting system of a company must be comprehensive enough to provide details of:

(1) sales made by the company;
(2) amounts owed to the company in respect of these sales;
(3) payments and receipts through the bank account;
(4) assets owned by the company;
(5) purchases made by the company;
(6) amounts owed by the company in respect of these purchases;
(7) wages paid, together with tax and other deductions made from employees.

These requirements are defined for a company by the Companies Acts, which provide the legislation for the protection of all parties dealing with the company and ensure that the company will be able to prepare accounts at the end of the accounting period.

These requirements of a double entry bookkeeping system will be satisfied in the majority of cases by a system containing the following:

Cash book

The cash book records all the transactions through the bank (despite the name 'cash book') and is the single most important part of the records. It has two sides on each page, the left (or debit) showing the amounts received by the company, and the right (credit) showing all payments made by the company. Each side will be divided into columns, with headings for the types of payments or receipts.

Sales ledger

A sales ledger is a collection of 'credit accounts' which customers hold with the company. When a sales invoice is raised and sent to a customer, the amount and details are entered on the debit side of the customer's account. When the customer pays, an entry is made of cash received, on the credit side of the account, which should be the same amount as the outstanding invoice if the customer has paid the full amount. A corresponding entry is then made on the debit side of the cash book for the cash received.

Sales daybook

The sales daybook is a record of all sales invoices issued by the business, in date order, usually grouped into months. The entry on the debit side of the appropriate sales ledger customer's account is a repetition of the sales daybook entry for the invoice.

Also required are a purchase daybook and a purchase ledger, which are similar to their sales equivalent.

Purchase ledger

A purchase ledger is a collection of 'credit accounts' which the company holds with its suppliers. When a purchase invoice is received from a supplier, the amount and details are entered on the credit side of the supplier's account. When the company pays the supplier, an entry is made of the cash paid, on the debit side of the account, which should be the same amount as the outstanding invoice.

A corresponding entry is also made on the credit side of the cash book for the cash paid.

Purchase daybook

The purchase daybook is a record of all purchase invoices received by the company, in date order, and usually grouped into months. The entry on the credit side of the appropriate purchase ledger account is a repetition of the purchase daybook entry for the invoice.

Once the business is expanding, it is advisable to employ a professional bookkeeper, who will keep the books up to date, fill in VAT returns and run the Pay As You Earn (PAYE) wages system. All this may sound daunting, but in practice the records which need to be kept are not complicated.

Without these records, the directors would have little idea of the company's performance.

The availability of immediate, accurate accounting information is an essential element of the success of any company.

Time-limits *

The books and invoices relating to the transactions of the company must be kept safe for many years after the period to which they relate.

Current time-limit requirements are as follows:

(1)   HM Customs & Excise (VAT) – 6 years
(2)   Inland Revenue (PAYE and tax) – 7 years
(3)   General accounting records – 6 years
(4)   Department for Work and Pensions – 3 years

It is important therefore to keep all the company's accounting records safe for 7 years.

The different types of accounts

When the company has started to trade, the directors will need to prepare accounts on a regular basis. There are two basic types of accounts, *management accounts* and *statutory accounts*.

These two types of accounts are prepared for different reasons. Management accounts are prepared on a regular basis (usually monthly) as trading continues. They provide the directors with information about the performance of the company.

Statutory accounts are required by law and usually prepared each year. A copy of extracts from these accounts or, for larger companies, a full set of accounts, signed in accordance with the Companies Acts by the directors has to be lodged each year at Companies House in Cardiff, Edinburgh or Belfast, depending on where the company is registered, and the public have the right to inspect these accounts and take copies. The public have no access to management accounts. The two types of accounts are now described in more detail.

Management accounts

Once the company starts to grow, it will become more important to know exactly how things are going on a regular basis.

Management accounts are simple accounts, normally prepared in-house, although in the early stages they may be prepared by the company's auditors where the company does not employ an in-house accountant.

The accounts will show sales, cost of sales, overheads and the profit (or loss) for a set period of, for example, a month. Then the next month another set of accounts will be prepared and the results may be compared, giving the management invaluable information with which they can manage the business more efficiently.

As things become more sophisticated, the management accounts may include:

(1) departmental or divisional analysis of results;
(2) comparison with preset budgets and variance analysis;
(3) accounting ratios and 'benchmarks'.

Typical accounting ratios used would be:

(a) Gross profit margin, ie $\dfrac{\text{gross profit}}{\text{sales}} \times 100$

which is a crucial ratio, indicating the percentage of profit generated from sales after deducting the direct cost of those sales. This 'gross profit' is then used to absorb the company's overheads, any balance of profit still available after overheads being the company's net profit.

(b) Current ratio, ie $\dfrac{\text{current assets}}{\text{current liabilities}} \times 100$

which provides an indication of the short- to medium-term cash flow strength of the company *at the balance sheet date*. It assumes that all current assets are convertible into cash in the short to medium term, ie within 12 months.

(c) Quick ratio, ie $\dfrac{(\text{current assets}) - (\text{stock})}{\text{current liabilities}} \times 100$

This ratio refines the current ratio to assets and liabilities which will produce imminent, rather than short- to medium-term cash flow *at the balance sheet date* and produces a critical and highly realistic indication of the company's ability to meet its immediate liabilities.

There are many more ratios, covering aspects from stock turnover to net profit margin. Indeed, accounting ratio analysis is a complete subject in itself. The director may wish to calculate a set of ratios which are particularly relevant to the individual company and the recommended course of action is to discuss the subject with the company's auditors or accountants, in order to decide exactly which ratios are the most relevant and should be produced on a monthly basis, as an appendix to the management accounts.

This core financial data provided by management accounts may be supplemented by other types of information to give managers a fuller picture of the company's performance. For instance, in a manufacturing company the management would review production reports, statistics, wastage data and efficiency figures.

Management accounts are of no use if they are out of date, and it is therefore very important to have a monthly deadline (for monthly accounts), of for instance the eighth day of the month, by which date the accounts must be completed and can then be reviewed by the management. Any changes which are then considered necessary as a result of the discussions may be implemented straight away. The effects of these changes will then be reflected in the management accounts prepared for the subsequent months.

Logical and efficient computerisation of an accounting system will make the production of management accounts far quicker and simpler, but caution must be exercised in this area. This topic is discussed in greater detail later in this chapter.

Statutory accounts **

Each year, a company is required to produce a set of statutory accounts. These accounts are similar to management accounts, but are normally more accurate, and disclose more information, or a different type of information. They must be filed at Companies House each year and provide the public with regulated access to the affairs of the company.

Some companies' accounts must be audited by a registered auditor (see Figure 10). The auditor must examine the accounts and underlying accounting records, and report as to whether in his opinion the statutory accounts constitute a true and fair view of the state of the company and results for the period.

The auditor often takes the opportunity available during the course of the audit to make some useful suggestions as to how the company may be able to improve profitability or increase efficiency. The directors of a company are under a statutory obligation to provide the auditor with whatever information he may require which is relevant to his audit of the company's accounts.

However, at the smaller end of the scale, a company may be

(1) totally exempt from the requirement to appoint auditors because it is a 'dormant' company; or
(2) totally exempt from the requirement that the accounts be audited because it is a 'small' company.

Many companies will qualify as both dormant and audit exempt companies, and will have a choice as to their route to audit exemption. Since the 'dormant' company rules require the shareholders of the company to pass a special resolution but the 'small' company rules do not, the latter route is usually preferable.

Format of statutory accounts

The statutory accounts must present the information in a standard way, as laid out in the most recent Companies Act in force at the time.

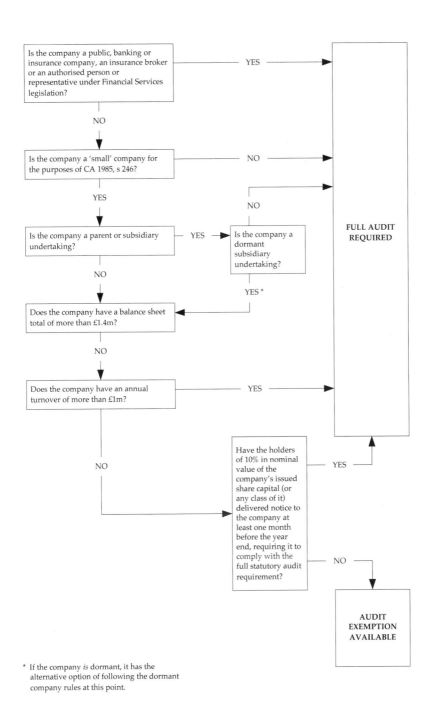

* If the company *is* dormant, it has the
  alternative option of following the dormant
  company rules at this point.

Figure 10 – Audit requirement checklist

The accounts will normally consist of:

(1) balance sheet at the accounting reference date;
(2) profit and loss account for the accounting period;
(3) cash-flow statement;
(4) notes to the accounts,

although smaller companies may only need to file extracts from the above.

Balance sheet

The balance sheet is a statement setting out all the assets and liabilities of a company at a particular date. A typical format will be:

	£	£
Fixed assets		10,000
Current assets		
Stock	5,000	
Trade debtors	22,500	
Prepayments	3,000	
Cash at bank/in hand	1,500	
	32,000	
Current liabilities		
Trade creditors	23,500	
Corporation tax	1,000	
Other taxes	2,500	
Other creditors and accruals	2,000	
	29,000	
Net current assets		3,000
Total assets less current liabilities		13,000
Creditors due after more than one year		(2,500)
		10,500
Capital and reserves		
Called up share capital		1,000
Profit and loss account		9,500
		10,500

Notes to the balance sheet

Fixed assets represent the cost (or later valuation) of all fixed asset items – land and buildings, plant and equipment, vehicles, less the depreciation written off the cost up to the date of the balance sheet.

Current assets are defined as all assets due to be collected within 12 months.

Stock is the trading stock the company is holding at the balance sheet date and is normally stated at the lower of cost or net realisable value.

Trade debtors are the amounts (including VAT) which the company is owed in respect of sales invoices raised which have not yet been paid, or to put it another way, the balance on the company's sales ledger at that date.

Cash at bank will be the balance per the company's bank statement at that date, reconciled to include any cheques written or amounts paid in which have not yet been debited or credited to the company's bank account.

Current liabilities are all amounts which the company owes which are due to be settled within the next 12 months.

Trade creditors are the amount the company owes to suppliers and is the opposite of trade debtors, ie the total amount outstanding on the company's purchase ledger at that date (including VAT).

Corporation tax will be any corporation tax the company owes, including that on the current period's profit.

Other taxes represent the total of VAT due to HM Customs & Excise and PAYE and national insurance contributions deducted from employees and not yet paid over to the Inland Revenue.

Other creditors are any other items owed by the company which do not fall into any of the above categories.

Creditors due after more than one year are required by the legislation to be shown separately in order to help a reader of the accounts assess the short and longer-term strength of a company in cash flow terms. Items appearing under this heading will normally be liabilities such as hire purchase balances, or long-term bank loans.

Called up share capital represents the cost of shares issued by the company to its shareholders.

The *profit and loss account* balance will be the total profit generated during the period, as calculated in the detailed profit and loss account statement, together with any balance of profit brought forward from previous periods.

A change in assets of a company from one period end to the next is represented on this side of the balance sheet by a change in the total balance in profit and loss account carried forward. The top half of the balance sheet, however, shows how the profit which has been generated has been retained or used – for example it may be in the bank as funds in hand, or it may have been spent on renewing fixed assets.

It is possible for small companies (see p 110) to prepare and file a reduced version of this typical balance sheet.

Profit and loss account

The profit and loss account is a summary of all the transactions taking place during an accounting period.

All amounts are shown without VAT, therefore representing the actual cost to the company (as the net of VAT received on sales and VAT incurred on expenditure is paid across to HM Customs & Excise by the company).

A typical profit and loss account for a retail company would be as follows:

	£	£
Sales		100,000
Cost of sales		
Opening stock	5,000	
Purchases for resale	50,000	
	55,000	
Less closing stock	5,000	50,000
Gross profit		50,000
Less overheads		
Wages and national insurance contributions	20,000	
Rent and rates	6,000	
Insurance	1,000	
Telephone	1,000	
Motor expenses	3,000	
Printing and advertising	2,000	
Sundry expenses	2,500	
Depreciation (etc)	5,000	
		40,500
Net profit for the period		9,500

Notes to the profit and loss account

All figures are net of VAT.

Sales are the sales made during the period, including those unpaid at the end of the period (ie debtors).

Cost of sales is the cost of purchases of goods for resale, adjusted to take account of the opening and closing stocks. The closing stock figure must of course be deducted, because that stock has not been sold during the period and therefore should not form part of the cost of sales figure.

Gross profit is a very important figure, because from it can be deduced the margin the company is achieving on sales. When divided into the figure for sales and converted into a percentage it forms a critical ratio when reviewing the results.

Overheads represent all other purchases made by the company during the period for items which are not directly for resale or involved in the manufacture of goods for resale. The overheads will sometimes be sub-grouped into categories such as finance, factory and marketing overheads.

Net profit is the difference between gross profit earned on sales and the overhead expenses incurred in creating those sales. This figure is then transferred to the balance sheet as above (after deducting corporation tax due on that profit).

Cash-flow statement

Required to be prepared only by medium and large companies (see p 110) and those companies regulated under the Financial Services Act 1986. This statement replaces the previous Statement of Source and Application of Funds and sets out the cash generated by the company in the period and how it was distributed or spent.

Notes to the accounts

Following the above statements in a set of statutory accounts there will be a series of notes giving a breakdown of certain items in the accounts, such as fixed assets, debtors and creditors.

What is an audit? **

An audit is a review of a set of accounts, and examination of the underlying accounting records from which they were prepared.

The auditor will either be presented with a set of accounts to audit, if the company has prepared the accounts itself, or in the case of a smaller company, he will probably prepare them from the accounting records and perform his auditing work as part of the process. The auditor will check all the figures in the accounts, not only to ensure that they are correctly classified (eg incorrect analysis of expenses, or items of a capital nature being written off in the profit and loss account), but also to satisfy himself that the figures are not over or understated.

He will, for example, review the system which produces a figure for total sales made in the period, and should go back through the system to make sure that it is watertight and would not produce an inaccurate sales figure.

He will conduct a similar type of exercise on the different sections of the accounts until he has satisfied himself that the accounts give a fair representation of what has happened during the period.

When the audit is complete, the auditor attaches his certificate to the accounts, which he signs. This certificate is called the audit report and states that the accounts give a true and fair view of the state of the company at the balance sheet date and also that the profit and loss account gives a true and fair view of the events and trading which has been transacted during the accounting period.

If the auditor is unhappy about any area in the accounts, then he is obliged to refer to this in his audit report if he feels that the matter is important enough. In extreme cases, the auditor may not be able to agree that the accounts are correct and will say so in his report. This situation is unusual in practice.

There are two types of audit report. The first, where the report refers to any problem or brings attention to a certain point, is called a qualified audit report. The second, the simple report, where the auditor agrees that the accounts are true and fair is generally referred to as a 'clean' audit report.

Distribution and filing of accounts **

When the statutory accounts have been prepared and, if required, audited or made the subject of a compilation report, they are put before a meeting of the company and approved by the shareholders, unless, in the case of a private company, the shareholders have passed an elective resolution to dispense with the requirement to put the accounts before a meeting. If so, the accounts will instead be sent to the shareholders. Once this has been done a copy of the accounts, signed by the directors, in accordance with the Companies Acts, is submitted to Companies House to be filed on record for the public to inspect if they wish. For a private company, the accounts must reach Companies House within 10 months of the balance sheet date. For a public company, the time-limit is 7 months.

A copy of the accounts is also distributed to each of the shareholders in the company for their retention.

Exemptions from filing full accounts for smaller companies **

Companies with a low turnover figure and a small number of employees are able to send only part of their accounts to Companies House to be filed. These are called 'abbreviated accounts'. The obvious advantage of this is that a limited amount of information is then available to any person inspecting the accounts by way of a company search at Companies House.

Smaller companies are categorised as either small or medium-sized in order to determine which parts of the accounts must be filed at Companies House.

A small company must satisfy two of the following three requirements:

(1)   turnover – not more than £2.8m;
(2)   balance sheet total – not more than £1.4m;
(3)   number of employees – not more than 50.

No profit or loss account, directors' report or cashflow statement needs to be filed for a small company, and only a simplified balance sheet and a few main notes to the accounts are required to be submitted.

A medium-sized company must satisfy two of the following three requirements:

(1)   turnover – not more than £11.2m;
(2)   balance sheet total – not more than £5.6m;
(3)   number of employees – not more than 250.

A profit and loss account must be filed by a medium-sized company, but this may be modified to omit turnover and cost of sales figures. The rest of the accounts are as normally required with a small exception of the note analysing turnover by geographical area and type of business.

The most likely type of people to carry out a search on a company will be the company's competitors and suppliers, in an attempt to establish the financial standing and credit-worthiness of the company. If the directors wish their suppliers to see the accounts, which is not uncommon when a company applies for credit facilities, then the directors may supply a fuller set of the accounts themselves.

Accounting periods

An 'accounting period' is the period of time for which a company prepares accounts, consisting of a balance sheet, profit and loss account, notes to the accounts and, normally, a statement of source and application of funds.

The term 'accounting period' is generally used when describing the statutory accounts of the company rather than other types of accounts such as monthly management accounts. The length of an accounting period must not exceed 18 months or be less than 6 months and will normally be 12 months.

The choice of accounting period end *

Choosing an accounting period end or 'year end date' as it is known, is one of the first tasks to face the new company.

Unless the directors notify the registrar of companies of a different date, the accounting reference date of the company in each year will be fixed automatically by the registrar as the anniversary of the last day of the month in which the company was incorporated.

Logically, the end of the first accounting reference period will be a month end date around one year from the date the company starts to trade, although if the company has a significant gap between the date it was incorporated and starting to trade, care must be taken to ensure that the first accounting period is not longer than 18 months.

Other factors may influence the choice such as a trade which is seasonal, where it would be sensible to end the accounting period at the end of the season. In this way, each set of accounts will show the results of one complete season and allow a meaningful comparison of results from one year to the next.

Administrative considerations can also be important, with many companies arranging for their accounting period end to fall at what is traditionally a quiet time of the year, such as early spring in retailing. This makes it possible for adequate resources to be allocated to the preparation of accounts, stocktaking and other year end procedures.

Changing the accounting period **

It is possible to change (ie shorten or lengthen) the accounting period of a company in certain cases by completion and submission of the appropriate form to the registrar of companies, although rules exist which restrict the ability to extend a current accounting period more than once within a 5-year period or to change an accounting reference date retrospectively.

Computers and accounting records

When the company has been trading for some time, the volume of transactions will rise, as will the amount of work required to maintain the accounting records. With the changes in technology that have taken place within the last 5 to 10 years, computers and software packages are now within the reach of even the smallest of companies.

It will normally be possible to convert the manual accounting records into a computerised system with minimal time loss and upheaval. Standard software packages are available on the market, ranging from simple systems for a few hundred pounds, which will maintain all the accounting records and provide reasonably sophisticated management information, to highly complex packages for a multi-national, multi-currency group of companies.

Hardware is also available at very reasonable cost, with industry standard computers now widespread and supplied with good backup facilities. However, caution is required in selecting computer equipment.

For those who are new to computers, it is essential to learn the basics. One method of achieving this is to attend a course designed for beginners, of which many are available. With an understanding of how a computer works, and how to solve simple problems when they arise (as they almost inevitably will) every director will be able to confidently tackle simple computerisation of his company's accounting system.

Choosing an accounting package **

This is an area where it is necessary to seek advice. The majority of practising accountants who deal with the smaller company should be conversant to some extent with the accounting software available on the market. There are a few fundamental questions which should be addressed before either hardware or software is purchased.

(1) What are the company's accounting system requirements? Is it a specialised trade requiring unusual software?
(2) What information does the management require from the system? This will be more comprehensive and more quickly produced than was possible with the manual system.
(3) Do the staff have the knowledge to run the system? If not they should receive training or a computer literate member of staff should be recruited.
(4) What is the company's budget for the exercise? It is essential to set a realistic budget and stick to it, otherwise the cost will almost always increase, as refinements are added and additional features are

included, which may not be necessary. The cost of small- to medium-sized accounting packages can range from around £1,000 to over £20,000.

(5) Will the system still be satisfactory in 3 to 5 years' time, considering the company's expansion and diversification plans? Ensure that the system is expandable or can be upgraded to the supplier's larger package.

These are just a few of the points to consider in the implementation of a computer system. Advice should be sought at the earliest possible stage, in order to ensure success.

Spreadsheets and databases

A spreadsheet on a PC is also a very useful tool for the production of management accounts and reports, as the structure of a report or a set of accounts will, in the majority of cases, be similar or identical each time it is produced. The spreadsheet packages available today are, on the whole, easy to use, powerful and represent good value for money.

Databases will be of use to the majority of businesses. They use the power of a computer to collect, assimilate and sort information in a fraction of the time the task would take manually.

There are many spreadsheet and database packages available on the market, some of which also incorporate word processors. Advice should be sought before committing to a particular package, as it will be very useful in practice to have a package which is well known and tested.

However, if a company is holding certain types of information about individuals, then it may be obliged to register with the Information Commissioner – see Appendix A for the address and telephone number of the Information Commissioner's Office.

Combined packages **

As software becomes more sophisticated, combined software packages are becoming available. These use a common database (holding customer, supplier and company information) which serves a number of software packages – typically accounting, CRM (marketing and contact management software), supplier and purchasing software and, increasingly, email.

Application service providers (ASP)

The term ASP generally refers to the rental of software or services over the internet. This is a slowly maturing market, but within the next few years it will be possible for a business to run all (or most) of its software applications, including accounting, over the internet using a remote ASP.

CHAPTER 10

Borrowing and Charges

Types of borrowing **

Companies frequently raise money by borrowing. The borrowing can take various forms. For example, 'unsecured loans' are simply contracts between the lender and the company for the loan by the lender and repayment by the company of a sum of money. Here, no mortgage or charge is given to the lender. A company may have a bank overdraft, and a mortgage or charge over the company's property is not usually required. However, borrowing is more likely to be 'secured' – the company will grant the lender a mortgage or charge over the company's property. In this context, property does not only mean land and buildings.

Under the laws of England and Wales and Northern Ireland, a company can usually create a charge over anything it owns, such as plant, machinery, patents, etc, and the word 'property' therefore means everything the company owns, which is capable of being charged. The security given by a mortgage or charge is, of course, that the lender has the right to seize and sell charged property if the loan is not repaid. The words 'mortgage' and 'charge' can, generally, be treated as interchangeable. The word 'charge' is used in this chapter.

Since Scottish law of property is based on entirely different principles from those which apply in England and Wales and Northern Ireland, it follows that the law relating to mortgages, charges and other securities over Scottish property is also different.

Scottish law distinguishes between heritable property (ie land and certain interests in land), corporeal movables (goods, etc) and incorporeal movable rights (shares, life policies, etc). With the exception of the consideration of the objects and powers of the company and its directors, which are the same in both jurisdictions, this book does not attempt to deal with this specialist area, save to say that advice from a Scottish lawyer should always be sought on any matter relating to secured lending under Scottish law.

Legal and financial advice should always be sought in respect of borrowing, and creation of charges.

The objects and powers of the company **

Wherever it is registered, the company must have power to borrow and create charges in its memorandum. Trading companies have an implied power to borrow, but usually a company's memorandum gives it express power. The memorandum should also contain an express power for the company to create a charge over its property. A lender will always require to see express powers in the memorandum in both these respects. An appropriate clause should look something like this:

> 'To borrow and raise money in any manner and to secure the repayment of any money borrowed, raised or owing by mortgage, charge, standard security, lien or other security upon the whole or any part of the company's property or assets (whether present or future), including its uncalled capital, and also by a similar mortgage, charge, standard security, lien or security to secure and guarantee the performance by the company of any obligation or liability it may undertake or which may become binding on it.'

The directors and borrowing **

Usually, the directors of the company will exercise its powers to borrow and create charges. The articles will provide unlimited powers for the directors to act on the company's behalf in this respect. However, the directors should always check the articles, because the articles may provide that the directors' powers to borrow on behalf of the company are limited, or, alternatively, that they cannot be exercised without a resolution of the shareholders of the company or the consent of a particular class of shareholders. This may be the case with a company which does not have modern articles of association.

Types of charge **

Debenture

'Debenture' is the word usually used to describe the contract between a company and a lender when money is borrowed. A debenture does not necessarily create a charge at all. It may simply create or acknowledge an unsecured loan from the lender to the company. However, it usually creates at least a floating charge. Consequently, a lender, or a lawyer, may treat the words 'debenture' and 'floating charge' as interchangeable although it is not technically accurate to do so.

Fixed charge

A charge is a fixed charge if certain specific property, such as an office or factory, is subject to it. Such a charge is sometimes also called a 'specific charge'. Whilst property is subject to a fixed charge, the company can only sell, let or charge the property with the consent of the lender.

Floating charge

A floating charge is a charge over the company's property which does not specifically affect the charged property until some event happens which causes it to turn into a fixed charge. Until that happens, it merely hovers or floats over the company's property, like a cloud. Upon the happening of such an event, it attaches to the charged property, as if it had been created as a fixed or specific charge. The cloud drops. A lawyer would say that the floating charge has 'crystallised'. It will crystallise if, for example, the company goes into liquidation or a lender appoints a receiver because the company defaults in repaying a loan.

The advantage of a floating charge to the company is that it may usually buy and sell its property in the ordinary course of its business, even though the property it owns at any particular time is subject to the floating charge, at any time before the charge crystallises, and it may do so without the lender's consent. This is obviously of benefit to the company – it can borrow money without restricting its continued trading activity.

Register of charges *

The company must keep:

(1) A register of charges, to include details of all fixed or specific charges affecting the property of the company and all floating charges on any property of the company.
   The register gives, for each charge, a short description of the property charged, the amount borrowed under the charge and the names of the persons entitled to the charge.
(2) A copy of every instrument creating a charge.

Shareholders and creditors may inspect the register of charges and the copies of documents creating the charges and, if the company refuses to allow inspection, the court may compel immediate inspection. Anyone else can inspect the register on payment of a fee not exceeding 5p.

If a charge is created and no entry is made in the register, the officers of the company who know about and authorise or permit the failure to make the entry are liable to a fine.

The register of charges and copies of charge documents must be open for inspection each day during business hours for at least 2 hours.

Register of debenture holders

The Companies Acts do not require a register of debenture holders to be kept separately from the register of charges but if there is one, it must be kept at the company's registered office or at any other office of the company where the work of making it up is done. Much of the information in it will merely duplicate the register of charges.

The registrar of companies must be given notice of where the register of debenture holders (if any) is kept unless it has been kept at all times since it came into existence at the company's registered office.

It must be open for inspection by any registered debenture holder, and any shareholders of the company without fee, and by anyone else on payment of a fee not exceeding 5p. Registered debenture holders and shareholders may have copies of all or part of the register.

Registration with the registrar of companies ***

Particulars of certain charges created by companies registered in England and Wales or Northern Ireland must be delivered to the relevant registrar of companies within 21 days after the date of their creation.

If not registered, charges are void in certain circumstances, the money borrowed becomes repayable in certain circumstances, and the officers may be fined.

It is the company's duty to register the particulars of the charge but any interested person, such as the lender, may do so. If the company fails to register it the person taking the charge should register it. Currently, no fee is payable on lodgment of particulars of a charge.

Registration is effected by sending prescribed particulars of the charge on an official form, to the registrar of companies within 21 days from the date of creation of the charge.

If the company creates a charge, the directors and secretary should check that its professional advisers have not omitted to register the charge.

CHAPTER 11

Taxation

In the UK tax system, there are three main types of tax affecting companies, these being:

(1) corporation tax which is charged on the profits and gains of the company;
(2) value added tax which the company may be obliged to charge on the sales it makes to third parties;
(3) income tax, under the Pay As You Earn system, which is charged on wages and salaries which the company pays to its employees and directors.

Corporation tax

A limited company is a legal entity, a legal person. Just as an individual's income in any tax year (the tax year currently runs from 6 April in one year to 5 April the next year) is totalled up and then subject to income tax at the rates currently in force, so a company is also subject to tax on its profit and capital gains in an accounting period.

Profit

Profit is defined broadly as the difference between turnover (sales) and all the expenses which the company incurs in order to produce that turnover. This difference also represents the change in total assets of the company from the beginning of an accounting period to the end of the same accounting period.

*Which expenses can be deducted? ***

In order to arrive at the profit, as outlined above, the expenses of the company are deducted from the sales figure. Some expenses are allowed to be deducted from the sales to arrive at the profit (ie they are allowable deductions) and others are not. In practice, the categories of items which are not allowable deductions are few.

The tax legislation which controls this subject and defines an allowable deduction is complicated and this is an area where professional advice should be sought if there is any doubt as to the allowability of a particular item. There is, however, a fairly reliable 'rule of thumb', which may be applied on a day-to-day basis with respect to expenditure. If the expenditure is relevant to the trade being carried on by the company and is incurred with a view to creating sales, then it is probably allowable. The tax legislation is itself based on this general theory and this rule will be useful in any cases of doubt.

The most obvious allowable expenses of a company will be:

(1) cost of sales, purchases of goods used in the manufacturing process or in the provision of a service;
(2) rent, rates, heat, light and insurance for the business premises;
(3) wages and employer's national insurance contributions for all staff employed and working in the company;
(4) motor and transport expenses;
(5) other overheads, advertising, office supplies, training and recruitment costs, etc.

Entertainment expenses, directors' personal expenses and legal costs relating to capital expenditure are examples of expenses not allowable as deductions against trading profits.

Tax deduction for assets (capital allowances) **

There is an important distinction to explain at this point relating to assets and their treatment as far as deductibility for tax is concerned. If a company expends funds on overheads, such as rent and rates, or fuel for company vehicles, then that total amount expended is allowable against the profits (when arriving at a taxable profit) in the accounting period in which the overheads occurred.

This is not so in the case of assets purchased. An asset is an item of *capital* nature as distinct from an overhead which is a *revenue* expense. This description of expenditure as either capital or revenue is widely used in practice.

Whilst the whole of a revenue expense is allowed against the profits in the period incurred, the cost of capital items can only be offset against profit by a portion of the cost of the asset per year.

The accounts term for this deduction is *depreciation* whilst the tax equivalent is *capital allowance*, ie an allowance for a capital item. The rate at which the cost may be offset varies between types of asset, but for the majority of normal business assets – vehicles, plant, machinery, computers and so on – the rate is currently, and has been for some time, 25 per cent of the unused balance each year. The initial allowance, ie the percentage obtained in the year of purchase, may be higher than 25 per cent. These 'incentives to invest' when introduced are announced in the annual Budget.

EXAMPLE

A van costs £6,000. How much of this will be allowed against the company's profit in each of the first three years?

Year 1	Capital allowance =	£6,000	@ say 40%=	£2,400
Year 2	Capital allowance =	£6,000		
	less	£2,400		
	unused amount	£3,600	@ 25% =	£900
Year 3	Capital allowance =	£3,600		
	less	£900		
	unused amount	£2,700	@ 25% =	£675

and so on until the vehicle is scrapped or sold.

This is only a brief summary, outlining the difference between the tax treatment of capital and revenue expenditure. The capital allowance regulations can become complex in places but it is an area where intelligent planning may minimise or delay a company's tax liability.

If significant capital expenditure is planned, then consulting the company's accountant or tax adviser should prove to be a worthwhile exercise. The possible leasing of assets should also be considered when the acquisition of capital items is necessary.

How is the corporation tax calculated?

Once the taxable profits for the period have been established then the corporation tax may be calculated. In straightforward situations the corporation tax due will be the taxable profit, after deducting all allowable items of expenditure and adjusting for depreciation and capital allowances, multiplied by the corporation tax rate.

EXAMPLE

	£	£
Profit per accounts		10,000
Add: Depreciation charged	1,500	
Entertaining expenses included in profit and loss account	400	1,900
		11,900
Less: Capital allowances		1,200
Taxable profit		10,700

Corporation tax at, for example, 20% = £2,140

The corporation tax rate

There are currently three corporation tax rates, with the rate used depending on the amount of the taxable profits for the period. The rates are known as the starting rate, the small companies rate and the full rate. The starting rate applies to profits up to a very low figure (currently £10,000), with the small companies rate applied to the next band of profits up to another level, which in practice is fairly high when discussing a small family company.

If profits are above this figure, but below the threshold for the full rate, there is a formula to calculate a marginal rate for that level of profits. Above the full rate threshold, all the profits are charged at the full rate. All corporation tax, for companies formed after 1963, is payable in one instalment, 9 months after the end of the accounting period. So if the company's accounts are made up to 31 March, then the corporation tax due on the profits earned in that period will be payable on 1 January in the following year.

Pay and file

Since 1993, a new method of dealing with payment of corporation tax and submission of accounts has been in force. Prior to that date, accounts and computations were submitted to the Inland Revenue, and, assuming that these were agreed by the Inland Revenue, then an assessment to corporation tax was issued and the tax became payable 9 months after the accounting period end.

Under pay and file, the company is obliged, within 9 months as before, to settle the corporation tax due, based on its own calculation of the liability. No assessment will normally be issued by the Inland Revenue at this stage. Accounts in support of this figure must then be submitted to the Inland Revenue within 12 months of the end of the accounting period. In addition, a detailed return form is also submitted, which effectively replaces the computations which accompanied the accounts under the old system.

It can be seen that the Inland Revenue are taking a lead from HM Customs & Excise, with the onus falling on the taxpayer to recognise and calculate their liability within the time-limits. Detailed regulations provide for complications such as a change of accounting date, and as would be expected, the Inland Revenue has the power to charge interest and penalties on late settlement of taxation liabilities, or failure to submit returns by the due date.

Group taxation **

The taxation of a group of companies can be a very complicated area when the group becomes large and intricate, although in principle the concept is fairly straightforward, and similar to the taxation of a single company. Each company within the group prepares its own tax computation, based on the results in its own accounts, and sends this to the company's local tax office as normal.

The differences arise when there is a company in the group which has either made losses in the period or has overpaid corporation tax. The losses or overpayment may then be transferred to another company in the group and used against that company's profit or tax liability, as long as certain conditions have been met between the two companies on share ownership and accounting periods. This use of losses and surplus tax within a group is known as *group relief*.

Distributions ***

A dividend is a distribution of profit to shareholders in a company. Which shareholders receive a dividend will depend on the rights (to dividends) which those shares have. In a simple case, if 100 ordinary fully-paid shares are issued in a company, all with the same rights (as defined in the memorandum and articles of association of the company) then all the shareholders will receive the same amount of dividend, which will be one-hundredth of the total dividend to each share issued.

The dividend is deemed to have been received by the shareholder net of basic rate tax. Prior to 1999, a company was obliged to remit Advance Corporation Tax to the Inland Revenue in respect of dividends. This no longer applies.

Capital gains tax

Tax is charged on a company's capital gains in a slightly different way than for individuals. A limited company's taxable gains are included in the corporation tax computation and taxed at the corporation tax rate. A profit is generated by trading, ie buying and selling on a regular basis or providing a service to customers, whereas a gain is created by purchasing an asset as an investment, then selling that asset some time later at a higher price.

This distinction between profit and gains is a very important one as it determines the treatment of any income created.

One difference between the way that companies and individuals are chargeable to tax on capital gains is that individuals at present are allowed to make gains of a small amount in each tax year without paying capital gains tax on them, paying tax on the balance. The level of this 'annual exemption' for capital gains tax is announced in the Budget each year. Companies, however, pay tax on the whole of any chargeable gains with the calculations being included with the annual computation of taxable profits.

The more common assets which companies may dispose of to realise a chargeable gain would be:

(1) plant and machinery;
(2) land and buildings;
(3) investments in other companies (shares).

Allowable expenses when calculating the gain will be items such as legal charges on purchase and capital improvement expenditure (but not repairs). In addition, an indexation allowance is added to the original cost of the asset. This is calculated to represent the elements of the gain produced by inflation, which is not taxable.

Subject to certain conditions, tax payable on a capital gain may be deferred if the gain, or part of the gain is reinvested in another asset. Professional advice should be sought.

Value added tax (VAT)

When a limited company starts to trade, VAT must be considered. Introduced in 1971, and replacing the old purchase tax, VAT is collected and controlled by HM Customs & Excise, a government body quite separate from the Inland Revenue.

A company is obliged by law to register for VAT if the supplies made by the company are subject to VAT, and:

(1) turnover has exceeded a prescribed figure, the VAT threshold, in the preceding 12 months; or alternatively,
(2) if it is expected that the turnover will exceed the threshold within the forthcoming 30 days.

This means that the company *must* charge VAT on all those sales made which are subject to the tax.

In certain cases, where for instance all sales are zero-rated, as described below, a company may wish to register voluntarily, even if the level of turnover is below the threshold. It would then be able to reclaim all input tax paid on items purchased and would therefore benefit.

Once the company has registered for VAT it will receive a VAT registration number from HM Customs & Excise and must print this number on all sales invoices.

If a company is registered for VAT then it must charge VAT on all sales which are 'standard-rated' or 'VATable', to use the colloquial term. The sale of goods or provision of service, either or both of which will form turnover, dependent on the type of business involved, are categorised by legislation into three types:

(1) standard-rated, the rate is currently 17.5 per cent on the selling price;
(2) zero-rated, where VAT is charged at 0 per cent (ie not at all); but it is very important to distinguish between this and
(3) exempt, where VAT is not relevant and not *applied*.

If the supplies are all standard-rated, then the company must add VAT (known as output tax) at 17.5 per cent to all the sales invoices and may reclaim VAT on anything purchased which carries VAT (input tax).

If the supplies are zero-rated, then VAT is added to all the sales invoices at 0 per cent, and shown on the invoice, and the company may reclaim VAT on anything purchased to which VAT has been added.

The important distinction to make is if the supplies are exempt rather than zero-rated.

If the supplies are exempt, then VAT must not be charged (at any rate) on any sales made, and the company cannot reclaim any VAT which has been charged on purchases. If all the supplies are exempt, then the company will be unable to register for VAT.

It can get very complicated when some of the sales made are standard or zero-rated and some are exempt – it is necessary to separate the input tax on purchases which relate to the standard or zero-rated items and only reclaim VAT on those expenses.

It is often possible in this situation to agree with HM Customs & Excise to reclaim a fixed percentage of the input tax, which would usually be based on the percentage split of sales between exempt and the rest.

The excess VAT (output less input) is paid across to HM Customs & Excise on a VAT return, a pre-printed computer generated form which is completed and sent to HM Customs & Excise, usually quarterly, together with a company cheque for the tax due. Some types of business, ie those who make zero-rated supplies and reclaim all their input tax, will receive refunds on each return, and this will be paid automatically into the company bank account upon submission and acceptance of the return.

It is possible, for smaller companies, to pay VAT 'on account' each month, and at the end of the year to submit an annual return and settle the balance of VAT due.

Scale charges

If a company provides motor vehicles for use by employees on non business mileage, additional VAT must be paid each period. The amounts vary, according to the type of vehicle and advice should be sought.

Cash accounting scheme

If a company has to pay over the 'output' tax charged on sales invoices, and it has not actually been paid by the customer, cashflow can suffer, sometimes quite severely. For smaller companies, the cash accounting scheme relaxes the rules, and allows the company to only pay over the output VAT received during the VAT period from its customers. Of course if this scheme is adopted, then the same principle applies to 'input' tax on goods and services purchased.

Advice should be taken on this subject as the adoption of the scheme is not always beneficial and HM Customs & Excise apply the regulations and limits strictly.

Late returns **

Strict penalties exist regarding late registration, submission of late returns and underdeclaration. VAT is an area where much care is needed and professional advice will often be required.

VAT inspections

HM Customs & Excise have a team of inspectors who make regular visits to VAT-registered businesses, to inspect the accounting records and check the information shown on the returns. This is quite routine, and should not be a cause for concern, as long as the VAT returns have been completed correctly.

Income tax and pay as you earn

Income tax is applied to the earned and unearned income of individuals either in employment or in business as sole traders (ie self-employed). It also applies to a partnership, which is simply a group of more than one sole trader in business together. Each person in the UK is allowed to deduct specified amounts from his total income in each tax year before arriving at a figure for taxable income. The most common deductions would be as follows:

(1) Personal allowance

An amount amended each year in the annual Budget in late autumn. For each tax year, both men and women receive an allowance which may be used against earned income.

(2) Payments into pension schemes **

If payments into a pension scheme are made without tax relief being given at source then, subject to certain limits, which depend on the taxpayer's age and total pensionable income, the total of these pension contributions may be deducted from gross income before arriving at a taxable figure.

Other items are deductible, such as some maintenance payments, professional subscriptions and a few additional allowances in particular circumstances. **

Utilising independent taxation ***

Husbands and wives are taxed separately on all sources of income. Consideration should be given to transferring any income-bearing assets, such as shares or investment accounts, into the name of the spouse who has the least income. This ensures that allowances and the lower rate tax bands available to both parties are fully utilised.

Each spouse may also have to submit a separate tax return and can choose to keep their tax situation completely private from their spouse, if they so wish.

This is outside the intended scope of this book, and is a topic which should be discussed with an accountant in order that tax affairs may be organised as efficiently as possible.

The tax due is then calculated on the balance (taxable income) and a tax liability results. In the case of a person whose only income is from a job, tax will have been deducted from their salary (or wages) each time they receive their pay through the PAYE scheme, and they should have no further tax to pay on that income.

The PAYE scheme

The system of deducting an employee's tax at source each time the salary is paid is called PAYE (or Pay As You Earn). Every employer who pays staff wages is obliged to tax their employees' wages at source.

Each employer operates a separate PAYE scheme, which will have a unique reference number such as: 123/A4567 – where 123 identifies the tax office which controls the PAYE schemes within the particular geographical area, and the A4567 is the reference number of that company's PAYE file in the tax office. 123/A4567 is therefore this company's PAYE reference.

Obtaining a PAYE scheme

When the company starts to trade and employ staff, and this includes paid directors who are also employees of the company, the company must obtain a PAYE scheme. This is done by contacting the local Inland Revenue office and requesting that a scheme is set up for that company. The PAYE scheme is then supplied by the relevant district tax office and the employer receives, in addition to the company's PAYE reference number, a pack containing tax tables, pre-printed sheets for calculating the tax and national insurance contributions for each employee, and booklets giving clear instructions on how to run the PAYE scheme.

How does PAYE work?

Each employee is given a tax code by the relevant Inland Revenue PAYE district. A tax code is a figure representing the annual amount of earnings from this employment that the employee may earn before he pays tax on the balance. Each employee's tax code will have been arrived at generally by adding together all the allowances, pension payments made and adjusting the code for any penalty due for the provision of company cars and other benefits. The resulting figure will comprise the individual's tax-free income for that tax year.

Each pay period, the employer takes the gross pay of the employee and then deducts (for monthly pay periods), one-twelfth of the annual amount of tax-free pay, which will be one-twelfth of the tax code figure. The amount of tax due is then calculated on the balance of income, at lower, basic and higher rate bands (whichever are appropriate), and the resulting tax figure deducted from the gross pay, to arrive at the net pay.

The employee's national insurance contribution for the pay period at the rate currently in force is also deducted from the gross pay.

So the calculation will look like this:

	£
Gross pay for period	1,000
Tax-free pay for period	200
Taxable income	800
Income tax at, say, 25%	200
National insurance contribution at 9%	90
Total deductions	290
Net pay for period	710

The employee receives his net pay of £710 and has paid all his tax and national insurance on that income.

Employer's national insurance contributions

In addition to the employee paying national insurance contributions up to a certain limit, on his gross income, the employer also has to pay national insurance contributions. So the cost of employing staff to an employer is the total of:

gross pay + employer's national insurance contributions

Employer's national insurance contributions are calculated as a percentage of gross pay and must be included by an employer when calculating overall staff costs.

Tax tables

The tax-free pay, tax due and national insurance contribution, both employee's and employer's, are all calculated by the employer using tax tables, which are a collection of booklets containing ready reference tables, designed to make the calculation and operation of a PAYE scheme as easy as possible for the employer. The tables are automatically sent to each employer when the scheme is set up, each year or whenever any changes take place, which may happen from time to time during the tax year.

Paying the tax and national insurance contribution to the Inland Revenue

The employer, at each pay period will be holding an amount of money representing the tax and national insurance deducted from the employee's gross pay, together with the employer's national insurance due on that gross pay. This total sum must be sent in by the company each month, to the Collector of Taxes, which is the section of the Inland Revenue which collects all tax.

Late payments and returns **

It is important to ensure that monthly payments and annual returns arrive with the Collector of Taxes on time, as interest or penalties may be charged on any amounts which are paid late.

Part-time and casual workers ***

Great care must be taken when making any payments to part-time or casual workers as they may have other employment. Even though the amount of the employee's gross pay from your company may be, taken on its own, below the tax-free figure for the pay period, they may have other income against which their total allowances may have been set and therefore tax may in fact be due on the whole of their earnings from your company.

Reimbursement of expenses ***

This is another area where the greatest caution is required. Payments made to employees for reimbursement of expenses may be subject to tax and national insurance contributions. Any practice whereby a company makes such payments on a regular basis should be reviewed by the company's advisers before payments are made.

Dispensations

If the company needs to pay expenses on a regular basis, then it is advisable to approach the Inland Revenue and ask for the authority to make these payments. This is called a 'dispensation'. In order to grant this, the Inland Revenue will ask to review the company's accounting systems and will look carefully at the amounts the company proposes to pay and the reasons for payment. If it is satisfied, it will grant the dispensation, and as long as the company maintains its accounting systems to the same standard as at the time of the inspection, the dispensation should remain effective.

Failure to make deductions ***

If the employer fails to make deductions from any payment to an employee and later it is agreed that these deductions should have been made and then paid over to the Inland Revenue, the employer may be liable to pay the deductions (on top of the gross pay already paid to the employee) and could also be liable to penalties for failing to apply the PAYE regulations correctly.

It is also important to be aware of the distinction between 'employment' and 'self-employment' for PAYE and national insurance purposes. A company making payments for services rendered by a person on a regular basis must ensure that the person is registered with the Inland Revenue as self-employed. If this is not the case, and the Inland Revenue cannot recover the tax from that person, then they may assess the company for tax and national insurance as described above.

CHAPTER 12

Insolvency ***

Insolvency is an all-encompassing term for a subject which deals with what happens to a company when it has been trading at a loss rather than a profit and is now in a position where it is unable to meet its liabilities.

In the early 1980s the law of insolvency was substantially updated and consolidated. The result of this work was the insolvency legislation of 1986. The new law was necessary as it became apparent that the law in effect before the new legislation was not always suitable or able to cope with what was actually happening in the business world.

Scotland

Insolvency of companies registered in Scotland is the subject of specific legislation, and reference should accordingly be made to the legislation and to works on this subject for detailed information.

The effect of insolvency on a Scottish company and the procedures to be observed are broadly similar in Scotland, in England and Wales and in Northern Ireland.

However, it should be noted that application to the court to order a compulsory winding up is made by petition to the Court of Session (or, in the case of a relatively small company, the Sheriff Court where the registered office of the company is situated) in Scotland. In relation to receiverships, Scottish law provides that a chargeholder may only appoint a receiver if the charge is a floating charge.

The secured creditors of a Scottish company will often agree amongst themselves the order in which their securities are to rank, although there are statutory rules providing for the ranking of securities in the absence of such an agreement.

Although secured creditors can take action to recover their security on their own behalf, it is normal practice for the creditors to leave it to the liquidator, administrator or receiver (as the case may be) to realise the assets in question and pay the proceeds to the secured creditors in accordance with any ranking agreement or the statutory provisions.

Insolvency practitioners

Up until 1986, there had been no legal requirement for an accountant, business adviser or other person to have any formal qualification which allowed them to deal with the procedures involved when a company became insolvent. The new Act changed this weakness in the law and introduced a new title of insolvency practitioner for such people. Only licensed insolvency practitioners are now allowed to deal with such matters.

This change was necessary in order to ensure that advisers dealing with insolvency have the required experience, knowledge and professionalism to perform their duties to the highest standard. It is now an offence for anyone to deal with insolvency unless he is a licensed insolvency practitioner.

Insolvency practitioners are governed by the body which issued their licence, the principal bodies being the Institute of Chartered Accountants in England and Wales, the Department of Trade and Industry (DTI), The Law Society and the Insolvency Practitioners Association. Each body oversees the work its members carry out and provides a degree of control which did not previously exist.

What happens when a company is insolvent?

The different situations which may occur in insolvency are as follows.

Members' voluntary winding up ***

If a company has finished the task it was set up to do, and the shareholders no longer have any need to keep the company, then they would 'wind up' the company – that is close the company down officially. If any profit is still left in the company at the point the members decide to wind up the company, then this profit would be distributed in the form of a dividend. Any assets would also be distributed or disposed of and the proceeds also distributed. A useful example of this type of winding up is a company formed to mine a coal seam, which has now been emptied of coal, with no prospect of any further seams in the area. The company would then be closed down in accordance with the shareholders' plans. A declaration of solvency is required and advice should be sought.

Creditors' voluntary winding up

This situation would arise when a company has become insolvent, in other words, either it is unable to pay its debts as they fall due or alternatively the liabilities of the company exceed the assets.

The shareholders decide to wind the company up and they would appoint a liquidator (who must be a licensed insolvency practitioner). The creditors are then informed of the shareholders' intentions and the directors convene a meeting.

At this meeting they have the option to appoint another liquidator if the majority of creditors in value – in other words the weight of their vote is in proportion to how much the company owes them – so wish.

The liquidator appointed will then proceed to sell the assets of the company and pay the creditors from the proceeds in strict accordance with the order of payment laid down in the insolvency legislation. This order is set out below.

Compulsory winding up

A compulsory winding up can arise where either the shareholders or creditors of a company force a reluctant company into liquidation, by making an application to the High Court. Any shareholder, creditor or group of creditors can petition the court for an order to be granted, and if their petition is successful, then the Official Receiver, an officer of the DTI, is appointed liquidator.

The proceedings are costly, unpleasant and frequently will end in adverse reports being filed with the DTI on some or all of the directors. Sometimes, in a larger case, another liquidator may be appointed by the Official Receiver to deal with the practical aspects of the liquidation, but the reporting and disqualification aspects will always remain with the Official Receiver.

Administrative receivership

If a company has borrowed money from a bank or other lender, and as a condition of obtaining the borrowing the company has given that lender some type of security over the borrowing, which would usually be a debenture or charge over some of the company's assets, then the party holding the charge has the right to claim back the amount due to him, given certain circumstances.

The commencement of a receivership will be activated by the chargeholder giving the appropriate length of notice to the borrower and having done that in the correct manner he will appoint an administrative receiver to handle the matter. The receiver would normally be a licensed insolvency practitioner and will take control of the company with a view to realising assets of the company, the proceeds of which will be primarily for the benefit of the chargeholder. Any surplus funds arising from the disposal of these assets, after repaying the chargeholder and settling the receiver's expenses, will be either paid back to the company or passed across to a liquidator who may have been appointed as a result of the receivership of the company.

The receiver is also required, in a similar manner to the liquidator, to submit a report on the conduct of the directors to the DTI.

Administration order

If various creditors are dissatisfied with a company's performance, then one or more can apply to the court for an order to appoint an administrator. The administrator would take over the running of the company with the intention either to trade the company out of present difficulties or, alternatively, dispose of the company as a going concern. The company can also apply, on its own behalf, for this type of arrangement.

This is a comparatively new method of dealing with companies in difficulty, having only been introduced in 1986, and relatively few cases have actually been completed. One of the aims of this legislation is to provide the opportunity to avoid a liquidation, it can sometimes have tax advantages and of course avoids the stigma of a liquidation itself.

Corporate voluntary arrangements

This is a rare form of administration designed to allow the company and its creditors or shareholders to formulate an agreed plan and deal with a crisis. They could agree that all creditors be paid say 50p per £1 owed and forego the remaining balance due, in order to give the company a chance of survival. As long as the required majority agree and the plan is approved by the court, then an administrator will be appointed to implement matters. Having proceeded with the plan and achieved its objectives, the administrator (described as a Supervisor under this type of arrangement) will step back and leave the company to continue its business.

Order of payment in liquidation

The order in which the liabilities of a company in liquidation are settled is as follows.

(1) Preferential creditors – amounts due to the Crown (subject to any fixed charges – see (2) below). In most cases this will be the VAT due in respect of the last 6 months and any PAYE and national insurance contribution which had been deducted from employees during the 12 months prior to liquidation. Other preferential creditors will be certain amounts due by the company in respect of holiday pay and wages.

(2) Secured creditors – creditors who hold a charge, mortgage or debenture on any or all of the assets of the company. If the charge is fixed, then they rank before preferential creditors. A floating charge, however, ranks after both fixed charges creditors and preferential creditors. A common example of a fixed charge would be a bank which has a charge on the debtors of the company. For a more detailed discussion on charges, see Chapter 10.

(3) Unsecured creditors – the remaining creditors. These will consist of those parties that the company dealt with in the normal course of trade such as the company's trade suppliers, lenders of unsecured

loans and so on. Any amounts due to directors on their loan accounts also falls under the heading of unsecured creditors.

However, at the time of writing, the question of whether Crown debts should continue to enjoy preferential status is being reviewed by the Government.

The directors' actions ***

The liquidator also has a responsibility to submit a report to the DTI not only on every company he deals with but also on its account all acts by the directors, both past and present, and can include the activities of any persons who, although they may not be directors of the company at the time of liquidation, have been directors at any time in the 5 years prior to that date.

It is also worth noting that the definition of directors for this purpose also includes any person who may have been acting as a 'shadow' director, which may be relevant for example where a company is transferred into a spouse's name in an attempt to avoid this kind of problem.

If an adverse report is filed, then the Disqualification Unit of the DTI has the power to prosecute the director on the basis of the report, and may disqualify any persons involved from becoming a director of any other company for a period of up to 15 years.

In 1992, the Institute of Chartered Accountants in England and Wales approved a guidance note in respect of the reports to be made to the DTI Disqualification Unit by liquidators and other insolvency practitioners. These provide useful indicators to directors of danger areas in which their activities are particularly likely to attract censure if their company finds itself in trouble, and their conduct comes under scrutiny.

Wrongful trading ***

The liquidator can also bring an action for 'wrongful trading', where the company's trade was continued when the directors were aware, or ought to have been aware, that the company could not avoid insolvency, and a liquidation, and could not meet its forthcoming liabilities. This may lead to the directors being held responsible for all the company's debts. The liquidator can also bring an action for false accounting and other illegal acts, which is an awesome prospect. The responsibility of holding the post of a company director should not be treated lightly.

Ignorance of the company's affairs is no excuse – the law clearly requires the director to keep himself informed as to the company's affairs, so he can judge the state of the company at any time.

When making such a judgment, two tests will be applied to the director. First, he must meet the minimum standard reasonably to be expected of someone carrying out his functions. Simply by virtue of being a director, he will be expected, for example, to have some financial competence. A finance director will, however, be expected to have greater competence in this area than, say, a sales director. Secondly, if he has some additional skill, knowledge or experience over and above the usual standard, he is expected to apply it – he will be judged more harshly because of it.

Conclusion

The law of insolvency has been drafted with great care and with the hindsight of many years of practical experience. It is intended to protect, as far as possible, all parties who may suffer as a result of any company becoming insolvent. It is also designed to eliminate malpractice and illegal acts, and is ruthless on any directors or shadow directors who have behaved improperly.

It is clear that the company director must be acutely aware of his responsibilities, especially in the light of the powers available to insolvency practitioners and the DTI.

The law is also designed to assist companies in trouble, by utilising administration on voluntary arrangements, and should any director feel that his company may be in difficulty, then he should seek advice sooner rather than later, as invariably this will be to the company's advantage.

How to locate an insolvency practitioner

Most accountants in general practice will be able to put you in touch with a licensed insolvency practitioner. Alternatively, many of the larger firms of accountants have separate insolvency departments, staffed by licensed insolvency practitioners.

CHAPTER 13

Using Professionals

No company can expect to succeed without taking some sort of professional advice whenever this becomes necessary. Each different type of company will be run by individuals with knowledge and training in their own specialist subject. Should the occasion arise when they feel they are in need of assistance in an area which is unknown to them, then they should seek help and advice from a specialist in that field, just as their own customers will do from them. For example, the solicitor, when he encounters an accounting problem will seek the advice of a suitably qualified accountant as the solicitor's training and knowledge is not in that area. Equally, in another situation the roles of adviser and client will be reversed when the accountant needs some legal advice on a particular topic.

One area where the 'horses for courses' approach is crucial is when dealing with transactions or companies which require consideration of Scottish law. Advice from a qualified Scottish source is a must. A list of Scottish solicitors able to advise on company matters is available from the Law Society of Scotland. For accountants, contact the accountancy bodies whose addresses are given in Appendix A.

The economies of using professionals

Professional advisers such as accountants and solicitors have spent many years studying and training and will have passed professional examinations to enable them to establish their practice and provide a service to the public. In the majority of professions they will also have to be members of their own governing professional body and will probably be unauthorised to practise in their own name unless they have passed the relevant professional exams and undergone the required period of training in a professional environment.

Consequently, in the majority of cases, the professional adviser will be able to perform a task or provide an answer in a fraction of the time in which it would take his client to produce that same result, if indeed the client possessed the knowledge and experience to attempt the task at all.

Fees

Accountants, solicitors and other professionals are sometimes regarded as being expensive for the service that they provide. There is no doubt that in some cases a client may feel that he has been charged an excessive fee for work which has been carried out, and if this is the case then he should raise this point with his adviser and request a breakdown of the costs incurred in completion of the work involved.

It is of course good advice for a client to agree either a fixed fee, or a ceiling above which the costs cannot rise without prior agreement. Professional fees may also viewed on an 'opportunity cost' basis. If a director is able to produce income for his company of, say, £100 per hour, in doing whatever the company specialises in and the director needs advice on a legal matter, it is unlikely that it would be more cost effective for him to attempt to solve that legal problem himself in, say, 5 hours, when he could have earned £500 for the company during that same period of time.

If, instead, a solicitor were to be approached and asked for advice on the matter he would normally be able to solve the problem for the company in a fraction of the time, and his advice would (hopefully) cost substantially less than £500.

There is also no guarantee, if the first course of action were to be followed, that the director would have reached the correct conclusion, whereas with a professional adviser this should be the case and the client will, almost certainly, have the right of recourse should bad advice be given and damage result.

The types of professional advisers

There are many types of professional advisers, surveyors and valuers, architects, actuaries (who deal with pension funds and investments), patent and copyright experts, marketing and advertising specialists, independent financial advisers, computer consultants, and so on, but the three types of advisers which the new company will almost always require either immediately or in the first few months of trading will be an accountant, a solicitor and a bank manager.

Choosing your advisers

Accountants

Accountants operating 'in the high street' and providing advice to the public will be trading either as a sole practitioner, where only one accountant runs a practice with supporting staff (or to put it another way it is a firm with only one partner), or as a larger practice, where several accountants will have got together (ie entered into partnership with one another), and will probably trade under their collective names – eg Smith,

Jones & Co. This of course depends on how many partners there are in the firm. It is advisable when selecting an accountant to consult to ensure that the accountant is qualified. Such a professional should have the training and experience to deal with the company's and directors' affairs competently. There are several different types of qualification in accountancy – chartered accountants, certified accountants, cost and management accountants, etc, but the two qualified accountants most commonly found who are able to sign an audit report for a limited company are chartered or certified accountants.

In practice, most of the accountants trading as firms, and offering their services to the public are chartered, although there are a minority of certified firms also in existence.

What should an accountant do for the company?

The areas where an accountant will be of assistance to a limited company will be as follows:

(1) discussing the start up, assisting with forecasts and projections;
(2) providing help and advice in the raising of suitable finance for a venture;
(3) organising an accounting and management information system for the company;
(4) advising on taxation matters, both for the company and the directors on an ongoing basis;
(5) advising on VAT;
(6) discussing payroll, PAYE and national insurance systems, and the employment of staff generally;
(7) providing advice on an ongoing basis as the business starts to trade and expand;
(8) providing tax planning advice at periodic intervals;
(9) discussing computerisation, suggesting suitable software and hardware and outlining necessary controls to include in the accounting system;
(10) each accounting period preparing and/or auditing the statutory accounts of the company or providing a compilation report in respect of them (or, alternatively, advising as to exemptions from audit) and then discussing taxation and other matters arising from the accounts;
(11) acting as a 'sounding board' for ideas and potential projects as they arise;
(12) advising on action required when the company is in difficulty and recommending the appropriate course of action, for example consulting a licensed insolvency practitioner.

How should you choose an accountant?

Probably the best way to choose an accountant, if you have no one in mind, is to seek a recommendation.

This may be from someone else in business who is satisfied with the service that he is receiving from his accountant, or failing that from your solicitor or bank manager who will know of a good local firm with the knowledge and experience to be able to provide sound and up-to-date advice.

The choice will have to be an accountant who is qualified to audit the accounts of a limited company, or provide a compilation report, if appropriate, and will normally be either a chartered or certified accountant.

It would make good sense to use the same firm of accountants for all the services required as the overall service the company receives should be improved by the accountant being aware of all the different aspects of the company and directors.

Registered auditors and accountants

As mentioned above, one of the services that an accountant will provide to a limited company will be that of auditing or of carrying out the work required in order to provide a compilation report. Many companies are required to have their annual (or otherwise if the accounting reference date has been changed) accounts audited by a suitably qualified accountant who is registered as an auditor by his professional body. This is required under the Companies Act legislation, which governs all legal matters relating to limited companies. The majority of accountancy firms in practice will provide these services, indeed for many firms it accounts for a substantial percentage of their annual fee income.

Even if your company does not require an audit (see Chapter 9), it is likely that you will ask a qualified accountant to review (or prepare) the company's annual accounts and submit them to the registrar of companies. This will ensure that the accounts are prepared in the required format and should avoid problems (and the possibility of the company being fined).

Some directors may wish to have their annual accounts audited – despite the fact that an audit is not required under the relevant legislation – as it provides an external review of the company's finances and a level of comfort.

Solicitors

Your need for a solicitor will vary depending on what kind of business you are in, but there are several areas where a solicitor would advise a limited company and its directors.

(1) Forming a company, issuing shares, changing the name, etc. (In practice, most firms of accountants will also provide a company formation service.)

(2) Providing help and advice as to the capital structure of the company,

such as number and classes of issued shares, and the identity of the shareholders.

(3) Preparing service contracts for the directors, which is an important area, and one which should be addressed in the early stages of appointment.

(4) Providing help and advice in the raising of finance for a venture.

(5) Advising on individual planning for directors and shareholders in relation to possible death – wills, capital gains tax and inheritance tax, and the destination of any shares.

(6) Drafting special articles or a shareholders' agreement to cover special situations such as joint venture, quasi-partnership or deadlock companies.

(7) Advising on protection of 'intellectual property', such as trade or service marks, copyright, patents, designs, etc.

(8) Dealing with matters relating to credit control, debt collection and other litigation.

(9) Dealing with company secretarial matters such as minutes for meetings, company documents and statutory books.

(10) Dealing with the legal aspects of specific transactions, such as the company buying back its own shares.

(11) Dealing with the renting of property and leases, the purchase of property and conveyancing.

(12) Advising on regulatory and compliance requirements as to, for example, the giving of credit, and on requirements relating to obtaining licences to carry on certain businesses. This would include advice on Data Protection Act issues.

(13) Advising on redundancy, unfair or wrongful dismissal, maternity rights and other employment related matters, such as health and safety, discrimination.

(14) Drafting standard terms of business.

(15) Drafting contracts for any business/supply or agency agreements the company is to enter into.

(16) Advising on supply contracts, such as contracts to acquire computer systems.

(17) Drafting contracts for the purchase of businesses, and of the shares of other companies.

(18) Advising on action required when the company is in difficulty and recommending the appropriate course of action, for example, contacting a licensed insolvency practitioner.

Once again, choosing a solicitor will very often be the result of a recommendation, although many firms of solicitors will have specialist areas of knowledge. It is therefore important to ensure that the solicitor you select has experience of dealing with the affairs of limited companies. Some solicitors, for instance, deal mainly with non-commercial matters and may not have the necessary experience to provide all-round advice to a limited company. This point is more relevant when selecting a solicitor than when choosing an accountant.

Bank managers

This subject ties in closely with Chapter 10, which discusses the subject of borrowing generally, and the comments in that chapter will apply here also. Your choice of bank manager will depend to a large extent on what it is that you require from the bank. If your borrowing requirements are high, then you will be dealt with by a manager who is at a senior level within the bank and able to sanction that level of borrowing.

On the other hand, if you simply require a corporate (limited company) bank account, and also perhaps a deposit account, then your local manager who may have dealt with your personal banking for some time, will be your obvious choice – assuming that he grants your requests.

Some banks have a policy of not handling corporate accounts within smaller branches, which means you may be passed across or upwards in the bank's structure. If you do not feel happy with this arrangement, then it may be necessary for you to consider moving your business across to another bank, which does handle limited company accounts at local branch level.

The bank manager is normally very experienced in dealing with the affairs of business in general, and should prove to be a useful source of advice on a wide range of matters.

Dealing with a bank *

In many cases, the first approach to a bank will be in order to obtain funding for the company's activities. It is essential that any request for borrowing is presented in a correct and professional manner, as a bank will be influenced in their decision not only by the commercial sense of any project but also by the people involved in the project and the quality and professionalism of the presentation.

For this reason, if funding of any substance is sought from a bank it is necessary to prepare a business plan, which is a summary of the proposed project together with cash flow forecasts and projected accounts. The company's auditors and advisers should have experience in this field and will be able to assist not only in the preparation of the business plan but also in the presentation of the plan to the bank.

In some cases where funding is required, and depending on the risk and viability of the project, it will not be possible for the borrower to negotiate the most favourable terms between several banks. Indeed, in difficult situations it may be impossible to obtain finance at all.

In recent years, many of the high street banks have rationalised their lending criteria. The halcyon days of the local manager who knew each business in the town well and was able to provide loans and overdraft facilities with no reference to higher authority have disappeared in many high street banks.

With the more rigorous lending criteria currently in place in the majority of banks, it is often impossible to obtain funding (particularly for a new venture) without providing security (or collateral).

Bank managers are generally very experienced in assessing situations and appraising the potential success of business projects. They will not normally lend in high risk situations or without adequate security to support borrowings.

Complaining about professionals

Most professionals are subject to rules about the manner in which they deliver their services, and the basis upon which they can calculate their charges.

The Law Societies, in England and Wales, Scotland and Northern Ireland, offer one or more leaflets in respect of such matters, available from those bodies at their respective addresses as shown in Appendix A.

Further information as to the procedures for complaining about particular accountants can be obtained from their relevant professional body. The addresses of those of the main bodies are shown in Appendix A.

Conclusion

Professional advisers can be of invaluable assistance to a company, its directors and future success. Selected with care and used effectively, they will become an integral part of the growing company.

CHAPTER 14

The Internet and E-commerce

Introduction

The last few years of the 1990s saw the emergence in the UK of a new and remarkable form of communication – the Internet. With the ability to communicate through this new channel, every business was encouraged to build a website and trade on the Internet. Many vendors were promising that this exciting new medium would transform traditional commerce as they had known it for hundreds of years. But the majority of forecasts were subsequently proved to be overstated and very few businesses actually gained any significant commercial advantage from early use of the technology. The Internet is not an all-encompassing panacea, but neither should it be ignored. It does have real benefits and every business should consider how they could use the technology to improve its efficiency and profitability. This chapter provides an overview of the whole web-based arena and provides pointers as to where a business should take some action.

What is it all about?

It is useful, first, to distinguish between the Internet, and the World Wide Web (www).

The Internet is a general description for a worldwide network of hundreds and thousands of computers. A useful analogy is the road network in the UK. From one address in a town in one part of the country, it is possible to reach any other address, by using the network of roads, lanes or motorways. The most important factors in locating that destination successfully is to, first, know the exact address you are trying to reach and, secondly, know how to get there in the shortest time. The www is one facet of the Internet network, and the most commonly used by businesses and home users. It uses www as the first part of an address and can therefore be described as one particular set of addresses and links which uses the Internet network as its pathway to connect users.

There are two key elements to using the www as a form of communication. They are:

(1)   the network itself, with its various elements; and

(2)   the interface used to access the www, which is normally the web browser.

The network

Just as the road network consists of connections with different speeds (motorways, trunk roads and suburban links) so does the Internet. Each country is laid out with 'backbone' connections which are very fast, wide cables, and these high speed connections lead into numerous central junctions (Points of Presence) around that country. The countries of the world are also linked with high speed connections, both in the form of underground cables and satellite links. From the junctions in each country, lower speed connections are laid which eventually arrive at a single address. The main telecommunications companies normally provide the high speed connections, and are likely also to supply the link from that network directly to the door of the user.

Addresses

The analogy of every house having a unique address or postcode works well when applied to the www. Each computer which is connected to the www will have an address, which is normally shown as a series of numbers (eg 196.234.22.123). These numbers identify a location on the network which has been assigned to a particular computer. When a website address is typed into the browser (eg www.jordans.co.uk), the system converts this into numbers by locating the www address in one of many identical directories across the world and identifying the related numerical address. It then finds the quickest route to that address (and therefore computer) and connects the user's browser to that computer. The speed of the connection will be affected directly by the address look up speed, the 'width' of the cables being used to reach that address and the volume of traffic also trying to use those connections. Driving through a busy motorway junction at the peak of rush hour can be a slow and frustrating experience, and using the www at certain times of the day can be equally irritating. The speed of accessing the www is also affected by the rest of the world. As soon as the Americas start their business day (generally midday in the UK) there can be a noticeable decrease in speed when traversing the US www networks.

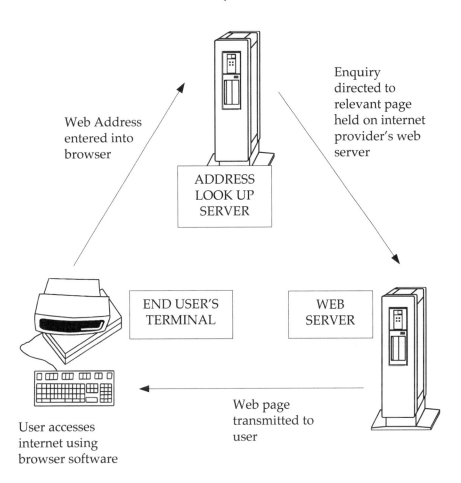

Address Look Up
Server converts
alphabetical URL (eg
www.address) into
numeric address of
internet provider

Enquiry
directed to
relevant page
held on internet
provider's web
server

Web Address
entered into
browser

ADDRESS
LOOK UP
SERVER

END USER'S
TERMINAL

WEB
SERVER

User accesses
internet using
browser software

Web page
transmitted to
user

Figure 11 – Basic structure of the internet

Web servers can be located anywhere on the globe and can hold hundreds of individual websites, each with their own unique numerical internet provider address (eg 193.130.81.82).

The web browser

The information collected when visiting another address on the www is written in particular computer code which can be translated into graphics by a web browser. The most common form of code used to write traditional web pages is HTML, and there are also many other more sophisticated software languages which can display moving images, produce sound and video images. A complex web page will be written using a number of different techniques and languages.

There are a number of web browsers available, but the most common are Microsoft Internet Explorer, which is supplied as a standard element of Microsoft Windows, and Netscape Navigator, its main competitor. These two products are used to surf the web by over 95 per cent of users.

The majority of websites (ie the code written to create the images) can be interpreted by both these browser products, although a minority of sites may not work with one or the other. This is either because the site is deliberately written not to work with one of the products or, more likely, the developers of the site have not considered the usability by both browsers when developing the code.

Email

Email has revolutionised communication since widespread adoption in the mid to late 1990s. This chapter does not deal with email in any detail, but it is useful to provide an overview of how a typical email system works.

As with the world wide web, it is based around addresses. Every email address will convert to a numerical address, in a similar way to the www. This numerical address will be that of a mail server, a computer which holds many email accounts (or postboxes). When a message is sent to an email address, the system forwards that message to the email server which corresponds to the numerical equivalent of the email address. The mail will then be collected, either by the email account holder dialling into that mailbox from their personal computer (as with the commonly used AOL or Yahoo mail accounts) or, in the case of a larger company, by the mail server automatically distributing the mail directly to the user's computer.

Mail is created using email software, which converts the mail into a specific language, recognised by the majority of other email software packages. In this way, mail created using one email package (eg Microsoft Outlook Express) can be read using another email package such as Eudora or AOL.

Individuals and smaller businesses are likely to use a dial up mail system, where their computer will dial into a centrally hosted mail server (or postal sorting office) and collect the mail. If the business has more than one mail user, the mail system at the user's end may then pass the mail through the business's internal computer network to the appropriate user's computer.

Larger organisations may have their own mail server on the company premises, which has its own mail address on the world wide network. The mail is then sent directly to that address (and therefore directly to the company premises) and again will be forwarded onto the individual user's computer.

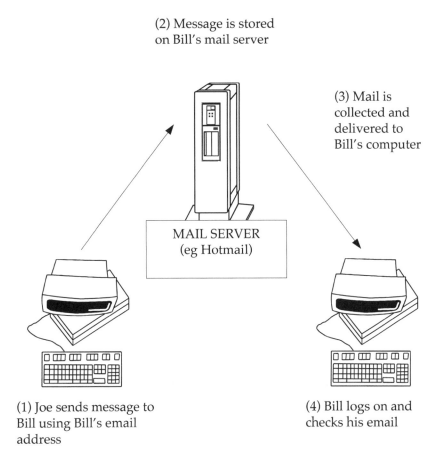

(2) Message is stored
on Bill's mail server

(3) Mail is
collected and
delivered to
Bill's computer

MAIL SERVER
(eg Hotmail)

(1) Joe sends message to
Bill using Bill's email
address

(4) Bill logs on and
checks his email

Figure 12 – How email works

This diagram shows how a simple email system works, as used by thousands of individuals who 'dial up' and collect their mail.

In larger companies, the mail server is actually managed by the company and will automatically deliver the mail to the relevant user's mailbox. When he logs on to the system, the mail will be waiting for him.

Using the technology to benefit your business

Effective use of the available technology can assist a business in a variety of ways. For many businesses, the expectation of increased revenues has not been fulfilled, and the opportunity to reduce costs is now seen by many observers as a more realistic benefit to be gained from correct implementation of the technology. It is important to approach this whole area with care and planning. A clear plan, which is compatible with the overall business strategy, developed and implemented in a logical and measured process, is likely to produce real, lasting benefits for most businesses.

The varying degrees of interaction

The most common areas where use of the technology will benefit a business are as follows:

(1) creating a presence;
(2) a marketing tool;
(3) providing information and assisting customers and prospects;
(4) improving the sales process and saving costs;
(5) communicating with suppliers and saving costs.

(1)   Creating a presence

The website will provide a simple point of contact through a web address, with brief details of the business, an overview of the operations and how to get in touch. It will probably contain a simple email link which will automatically create an email message from the web page and deliver it to the company email postbox. A large percentage of the smaller company websites created in the late 1990s go no further than this. It will add very little to the business but, in some cases, the strategy will determine that nothing more is needed.

(2)   A marketing tool

The site will be rich in design and impact. It will contain product or service information, details of satisfied customers with case studies, some history and information about the business and key locations and individuals, contact information and maps. It may contain a marketing survey which users can enter.

(3)   An information point

One of the most effective uses of the technology is to provide information to customers and prospects – used often by businesses which sell more complex products or services. The site may contain detailed data and information about products and services and it may be possible to download technical specifications, price lists and images of particular offerings. It may be necessary to pass through a 'Chinese wall', by entering a username and password to access some of this information which the company may not wish to be available to the public.

Many organisations are now experiencing real cost savings from the delivery of information and dealing with enquires through a structured process within their websites. They find that customers and new enquirers are often very happy to do the work themselves, browsing through catalogues and information, completing an online form to request information and downloading product details and images. For more information on online catalogues, go to www.actinic.com.

(4) *Improving the sales process*

The ability for customers to order goods and services online was forecast to revolutionise trading practices as we knew them. With a few exceptions, mostly in the B2C (business to consumer) market, most notably books and CDs (eg www.amazon.co.uk), this has not been the case. The reasons are complex, but the willingness of businesses in the early days to trade online was overestimated, the ease of completing a transaction was not dealt with adequately and, most importantly, the fact that business is in many cases a 'one to one' people transaction was ignored.

Huge investment also went into online exchanges, public (sometimes within an industry) locations where a business can visit and transact with other businesses in a similar market or requiring common goods. The majority of these early exchanges struggled to operate at a profit and many closed down. New exchanges have emerged, with better design and functionality and some will succeed. What has become clear is that online trading is suitable for some goods and services but not for others. Each business must decide if their processes and products would suit this method of transacting.

Online selling

STAGE 1

The first step on the ladder of online selling is to display a catalogue or list of products on the website. These may be organised into sections, to assist the user in finding what he needs, and there may be a search facility on the catalogue. Once the user has chosen a product, he may order this using a simple form (which creates an email message delivered to the business), which means that the business will have to respond manually and deal with the financial side of the transaction in the normal way. Alternatively, it is possible to link the catalogue system on the site into a system which will take the user's credit card details and carry out the transaction automatically. The third party 'transaction enabler' will then collect the funds from the online purchaser and remit them to the vendor, after deducting its fee, which will vary. A list of online transaction processors is shown at the end of this chapter.

Online selling in this way is simple but has disadvantages. The transaction is not automatically entered into the company accounting system, which means that it will have to be rekeyed internally. The product information on the website is static and will have to be amended manually every time a change is required.

Moving from this stage of online selling (which probably represents over 80 per cent of the online selling currently taking place on the www) into a more sophisticated, integrated model is a major step and requires significant planning and investment.

STAGE 2

There are a number of elements in the online selling process which can be linked into 'real live' information. Facilitating each of these may require significant investment in time and resource and the relative benefits of each should be carefully considered.

Customer details, price structures and habits

If a customer visits a website and the site recognises that customer (see personalisation and cookies in rule (6) of 'the eight golden rules of the web', below), then it can also offer that customer a bespoke set of products or process. The likelihood of that customer ordering goods online will increase if the ordering process is streamlined to fit in with that customer's requirements and past habits. If the site avoids the need for the customer to trawl through the same steps in locating the products he requires, then he is more likely to purchase. Many of the B2C supermarket sites attempt to do this by storing a list of favourites – goods which the customer purchases on a regular basis.

Product information

If the product details on a site are delivered real time from a live database, this not only ensures that the customer is viewing accurate information about the latest products, but also eliminates the need to update the website information and therefore saves ongoing costs. More sophisticated systems will not only generate live product details but may also interrogate stock systems and generate purchase orders online. They may also interrogate the credit account of a customer whilst the customer is viewing the website to determine whether that customer is able to order further product within the predefined credit limits.

Systems integration ***

Integrating product and customer details as described above will require complex database integration and can involve the business systems being accessed online, which creates many security and technical issues. In many cases, the long-term commercial benefits of this integration are likely to outweigh the required investment and cultural shift, but moving beyond a simple online ordering 'catalogue' processes will require detailed planning and must form an integral part of the overall business strategy. Specialist help will almost always be required. For more information on online transaction processors go to www.worldpay.com.

(5)   Communication with suppliers

If a business has made the investment to integrate internal systems with online selling or ordering processes, then it is likely that the integration of suppliers' transactions will be a less costly and painful step. In some cases (where the benefits can be seen more clearly on the purchasing side of the business), it may be beneficial to improve the supplier communication using web technology in advance of the customer areas.

One major change – replacing EDI

Just as customers may come onto a site and view products for sale, and then place an order, so a business may improve its purchasing function. For decades, many larger businesses have used Electronic Data Interchange (EDI) to place orders with smaller suppliers. This is often found in situations where one large purchaser, such as a major supermarket chain, would purchase from numerous smaller suppliers. The purchasing company would implement an EDI system and make it mandatory for all its suppliers to install the corresponding system and receive orders. Many EDI systems are not web-based and a significant number of smaller suppliers would not generally integrate the ordering system into their internal system, but simply receive an order through the EDI system and then process it in the traditional way. Many EDI systems are being replaced with web-based systems, which make it far easier for a large customer to reach suppliers using a common format and process. It is still likely that the recipient of the orders (the smaller supplier) may not integrate the orders received into its systems, as discussed above in relation to customer and product details, but a web-based ordering system enables the purchasing company to reach almost all the suppliers without the need for the suppliers to implement expensive EDI systems.

Online ordering for all

Outside the scope of the EDI arena, which only usually relates to a specific relationship between customer and supplier, is the concept of online tendering. A purchasing company can display details of the goods it requires, inducing the packaging requirements, delivery date and time, and detailed technical information about the products it requires. Suppliers can then visit the site, or receive automatic notification of a requirement being posted, and then submit their quotation to fulfil an order. The system can be open to all potential suppliers, or can be restricted, again through the process of usernames and passwords, to preferred suppliers. Most systems will have the facility for a new supplier to apply for registration, and these new suppliers would be vetted by the purchasing company before being issued with a username and password which enables them to access the site and submit quotations. Again, this system can become more and more sophisticated, with further systems integration enabling the production of delivery notes, purchase orders and, ultimately, transmitting the order instruction directly and seamlessly into the sales and delivery system of the supplying business. For more information about online ordering and supply chain, go to www.kineticnorth.com.

The eight golden rules of the web

There are eight golden rules that need to be borne in mind when investing in web-based technology.

(1) Focus on your customers – they are the lifeblood of the business.
(2) Avoid endless internal data. Pictures and CVs of key management are interesting and useful, but should be deep into the website, not on the first page a user finds.
(3) Capture your users' details. Whenever your website receives a visit, try to capture details of that visitor. Demanding pages of information about users will only cause irritation, but requesting an email address and some information, especially when the user has been in the site for some time and is clearly interested will probably not cause offence and will provide you with valuable prospect information.
(4) Ensure that the navigation is effective. Plan the pathway through your site carefully. Make sure that the homepage is accessible from every other page. Construct the navigation in a way that makes any place on the site accessible in three clicks or less. Ask third parties to test the site before you launch it and incorporate their comments.
(5) Keep load times down. Your audience will be accessing the site with differing download speeds. Work on the lowest common denominator. Make sure that images are compressed effectively. Aim for a maximum page load time of less than 10 seconds at the slowest access rate on every page. Make any plug-ins or complex offerings optional.
(6) Consider personalisation and cookies. The aim of every site is to increase the number of visits, the length of each visit and the commercial benefit gained from each visit. Requiring a user to 'log in' to all or selected areas of a site enables the site to recognise the user by downloading a small file (a cookie) onto the user's computer. The next time that user visits the site, it will recognise them and may greet them

with a 'hello John' message. This small piece of personalisation is thought to increase the user loyalty to the site and the likelihood of them using the site facilities and returning more often. More sophisticated sites will display differently constructed pages for each user, and may remember their habits from previous visits. Developments such as these can increase the cost of building a website substantially and, once again, the business benefits must be considered in comparison to the cost of implementation.

(7) Do not give your users unwelcome surprises. It is very frustrating for a user to, for example, complete a registration form which may involve 5 or 10 minutes' worth of work, and then at the very last screen be asked for something which they may not have access to immediately – or even worse advise the user that they will have to make a payment for the service. It is bad etiquette to use these techniques on websites and you will probably lose a customer for ever if you do so.

(8) Keep Flash (web software used to create animation) and similar tricks to a minimum. Unless your site is pure marketing, or you wish to convey your skills at creating complex and 'glitzy' websites, avoid the use of excessive animation. The majority of business users simply wish to access information and to do this quickly. The novelty of moving graphics and clever gizmos on a website is now passé.

Legal considerations

As we have seen, e-commerce – email and the web – can both benefit your business enormously. Email means you can communicate with customers, suppliers, creditors, the general public and other employees more easily and quickly. The web makes your business visible worldwide so you can create better trading relations with existing customers, attract customers in new markets, compete more effectively with your competitors and attract potential business partners.

Yet both also create dangers. Email creates a new way for you (or, more likely, an employee) to create contractual relations, defame third parties, sexually harass colleagues or make trade secrets available to competitors. Taking orders or communicating with suppliers or other business partners over the web can create legal issues that you need to address. You may find that your terms of business are inadequate – even unlawful – in the context of new customers you attract, or that those of your suppliers leave you exposed now that parts of your relationship are electronic. You may also need to consider settlement implications because you are being paid in a foreign currency for the first time.

Businesses selling similar goods or services under a similar trading style may become aware of your existence because of your website and take action against you. In many cases, existing law provides a framework for addressing these issues. It is simply a matter of applying familiar legal principles or rules to new circumstances. In other areas, new rules are needed because the law lags behind technological advances. It is in these areas that the greatest difficulties occur. The following points highlight the main areas to think about, but these are all areas where professional advice is strongly recommended.

Intellectual property issues

Trade marks ***

One form of intellectual property is the trade mark. Use of a name, logo or combination of both in relation to particular goods or services creates trade mark rights. The courts will allow the owner of a trade mark to sue another business in the courts for 'passing off' if that business is using the same or a similar mark in relation to similar goods or services in a way that is likely to damage the owner's business or goodwill.

If the owner has also registered the mark in a national trade mark Registry or under an international system, such as the European Community or Madrid Protocol system, the owner's rights are even easier to enforce.

However, some businesses may have used and registered a trade mark legitimately in the territories in which they have traditionally operated. If such a business establishes a website, the fact it is using a particular mark is instantly visible to potential customers in territories where the same mark may be legitimately owned and registered by another business. Unsurprisingly, the web has led to a rise in trade mark disputes.

Such disputes cannot always be resolved easily if they arise. When setting up a website, businesses therefore need current, expert advice on how to avoid or minimise the possibility of such disputes.

Domain names ***

Registration of a domain name gives a business surprisingly few rights and/or protections over and above those already conferred by trade mark law.

Domain names are administered by registries that operate under the auspices of the International Corporation for Assigned Names and Numbers (ICANN). Around 250 national registries offer registration under 'country code' domains like .fr (France) and .de (Germany). Others are international and offer registration under generic domains. These include the most popular domain, .com, administered by Verisign.

Some national registries offer registration under 'second level' domains. The UK registry, Nominet, is one of these. Applicants must register under one of the second level domains such as .co.uk or .ltd.uk, rather than directly under the .uk domain.

Traditionally, ICANN has allowed registries to set their own rules about who can register. A number do have rules that limit registrations to, for example, applicants with a local presence or a pre-existing registered trade mark. For example, widgets.ltd.uk could only be registered by a UK limited company called Widgets Limited.

However, these restrictions are few and far between. For example, while the .ltd.co domain is restricted, anyone can apply to register under the .co.uk domain. The same is true of the .com domain. These 'first come, first served' domains became a real problem for businesses who found their trade marks were being registered as domain names by cybersquatters – folk with no legitimate interest in a trade mark or other name who registered it and then tried to sell it back to those who did at exorbitant prices. It did not help that the unrestricted domains included the most popular ones.

This has meant that, generally, registering a name under one domain will prevent registration of an identical name under that domain but it does not often prevent either:

– registration of an identical name under a different domain; or
– registration of a similar name under the same domain.

For example, the fact that Widgets Limited has registered widgets.com would not prevent someone else registering widgets.co.uk, or even widgetsuk.com.

However, the tide is now turning in favour of owners of existing rights. First, ICANN has introduced a Uniform Dispute Resolution Procedure that has been adopted by the international registries and a number of the national registries. A trade mark owner (or anyone with a legitimate interest in a name) who is clearly a victim of cybersquatters can apply to have the domain name removed. The UDRP provides quick, easy resolution in clear-cut cases. Application fees are low and the procedure is written, so legal fees can be kept to a minimum.

Other registries have also developed, or are introducing, their own versions of the UDRP. These include the UK's own Nominet.

These procedures do not provide a solution in circumstances where two businesses are legitimately using the same or a similar name but only become aware of each other because of the web. In such circumstances the legal remedy is a passing off action in the courts, based on usual principles. In practice, the court is the last resort.

As well as the UDRP, there have been some moves towards protecting owners of existing rights against cybersquatters and other infringers at the registration stage. For example, with the introduction of new generic domains (such as .biz and .info in 2001), ICANN has started requiring the new registries to establish rules to protect businesses with existing rights in a name against abusers and/or infringers.

When considering domain name registration strategy – which domains to register under, which variations of names to register, what to do if cybersquatters have already registered your names, what to do if there are other legitimate users of your name already registered – professional, expert advice is vital both to provide as much protection as possible and to ensure that money is not wasted on unnecessary registrations.

Copyright issues ***

A business commissioning the design of a website from a third party should ensure that the copyright in the website design will belong to it, irrespective of the stage reached in that design. This should take the form of a written agreement between the business and the web designers whereby the designers grant copyright in its work to the business. Practically, the designers should also be asked to provide a copy of the design on completion, and at pre-determined stages during the development in case the work needs to be assigned to a different designer for any reason.

Compliance issues

Data protection ***

The Data Protection Act 1998 requires businesses that collect and use personal information about customers or other individuals to observe eight principles. The data must be:

(1) fairly and lawfully processed;
(2) processed for limited purposes;
(3) adequate, relevant and not excessive;
(4) accurate;
(5) not kept longer than necessary;
(6) processed in accordance with the individual's rights;
(7) secure;
(8) not transferred to countries without adequate protection.

Partners in a business partnership are treated as individuals for the purposes of protection under the Act.

The principles mean, for example, that data about an individual cannot be collected and used unless the individual consents, or it is necessary under a contract with the individual to fulfil a legal obligation or there is some other necessity. Clearly, websites that capture visitors' details must take this into account.

It also means that businesses must allow individuals access to that information and they can require correction or deletion of that information. The information does not have to be collected or stored electronically for the Act to apply.

One requirement of the Act that exercises businesses is that data collected for one purpose cannot be used for another without permission. For example, if a customer provides an address for the purpose of enabling an order to be processed, it cannot be used, for example, for an unrelated promotion by post unless the customer has consented to the data being used for other purposes. Website order forms should therefore ask customers for permission to use data for other purposes when taking orders online.

The Data Protection Act 1998 is a complex and far reaching piece of legislation that affects businesses far beyond their e-commerce activities. For more information, go to www.dataprotection.gov.uk

Contractual issues

Terms of business ***

The web provides a new means for customers to place orders, who may never have dealt with the business before. It therefore becomes important that they are specifically made aware of its terms of business before placing orders. This is because knowledge of, for example, limitations on the business's liability if something goes wrong will not be implied by a court without a course of dealing.

A simple precaution is to make sure that all customers ordering over the web see the terms of business. Many websites present customers placing an order with their terms of business and require the customer to click 'I agree' before confirming the order.

The web also opens businesses to markets beyond their national boundaries. Terms of business that are perfectly adequate for domestic markets may need revisiting for these wider markets.

For example, terms may need to provide specifically that it is the business's domestic courts that have jurisdiction in the event of a dispute, that payment must be made in sterling and that there are special credit terms for overseas orders.

The business may benefit if the terms tailor the rules of offer and acceptance for web orders. Offer and acceptance is necessary before a contract is concluded and the terms of business can dictate when this happens. For example, retailers usually provide in their terms of business that they are not making an offer to sell by putting priced goods on the shelves. If they were, a shopper could insist on the retailer selling incorrectly priced goods. Instead, the shopper makes an offer to buy at the checkout, and it is up to the retailer whether to accept the offer or not.

A business taking orders over the web may wish to provide that those orders are offers to buy (that the business can decide whether to accept or not when the order is received), rather than offers to sell that the customer can accept by placing the order.

Businesses may wish to provide in their terms that they will not accept orders from customers in certain countries. This can be one way to help avoid a trade mark dispute with a business in another country. Or it may be because that country has laws that protect customers – that provide cooling off periods, or override clauses in the terms of business that show liability – which are not acceptable to the business.

Particularly, EU businesses are affected by the EC Directive designed to protect consumers buying at a distance rather than face to face. In the UK, this has resulted in the Consumer Protection (Distance Selling) Regulations 2000, SI 2000/2334. These affect online purchases. More information about the Regulations is available at www.dti.gov.uk.

Businesses communicating electronically with suppliers and other business partners would also be well advised to review their trading contracts. For example, the possibility of security breaches that give outsiders access to confidential information may mean that your business will wish to reconsider the confidentiality clause in its contracts.

These are just examples of the issues that can arise. Businesses should get expert professional help in reviewing their terms of business for use online and keep them reviewed as the law develops in this fast changing area.

Employment issues

Employees – email and web use ***

In the past, businesses have been greatly exercised by the potential for misuse inherent in giving employees access to email and the web. This includes wasting time surfing or emailing, looking at pornographic or other offensive sites, defamation and harassment.

Such misuse can have serious implications for a business that has failed to consider how to prevent it. For example, employers can be prosecuted for failing to take sufficient care to stop one employee defaming another by email.

As both law and practice are fast moving in these respects, most businesses have not amended employment contracts to deal with them but have chosen to introduce email and web policies, usually as part of the staff handbook. Business lawyers now routinely draft such policies, tailored to the needs of particular businesses and their cultures. Alternatively, precedents are available on the web for businesses to download and tailor to their own needs.

Businesses wishing to take more draconian steps can take advantage of the Regulation of Investigatory Powers Act 2000, which allows employers to monitor email received and sent by employees. This is a thorny issue and legal advice is strongly recommended before taking this step.

CHAPTER 15

Further Considerations

Employees ***

The relationship between the company and its employees is governed by a substantial body of employment and other law. Questions of employment law should always be referred to the company's professional advisers. The law is complex and changes constantly.

The aim of this chapter is therefore to provide an aide-mémoire or check-list, rather than deal with detailed rules relating to any particular matter.

In order to establish the relationship of employer and employee there must be an agreement between the company and the employee, whereby the employee agrees to give services to the employer. It can be difficult to distinguish between the status of an employee and that of an independent contractor. A lawyer will say that the employee enters into a contract *of* service, and an independent contractor enters into a contract *for* services. The distinction can be very important. For example, under a legal rule called 'vicarious liability', an employer may be liable for loss or damage to others which is caused by his employee if in the course of his employment.

The contract between the company and employee does not have to be written. Sometimes, the law will impose additional terms on the employer and employee, which apply whether or not they want them to. For example, in relation to certain types of work or certain types of employee, or as a result of rules established by official bodies such as wages councils. The rules and customs of a particular industry may also apply automatically.

Other terms will be implied in relation to matters which the employer and employee may not have even considered. For example, there is a rule that an employer must pay the employee in cash. This prevents one practice of the nineteenth century, whereby employees were paid in tokens, which could only be spent in the employers' shops.

Whilst the contract need not be in writing, it is sensible to have a written contract for senior or important employees. The contents of the written contract should be very carefully considered, especially those clauses dealing with matters such as benefits in kind for the employee, and the company's right to stop the employee leaving the company and setting up in competition.

If there is no written contract, most employees must be given written information about the main terms of their contract with the employer. This is not a contract, but merely 'for information only'.

The written statement must be given within 2 months of the start of the employment. Some items which must be included are:

(1)   the names of the employer and employee;
(2)   the date employment commenced, and whether any period of employment with a previous employer counts for the purpose of determining 'continuous employment' (eg for redundancy calculations);
(3)   the rate of pay and whether pay is hourly, weekly, monthly, etc;
(4)   details of pension schemes, disciplinary rules, grievance procedures, etc.

It is possible to cross-refer to other documents, handbooks or manuals which are made available to the employee by the employer. Forms of written statement are available from legal stationers.

Not all employees are entitled to a written statement. Employees working less than 8 hours a week, spouses of the employer, civil servants, dockers and seamen do not have to be given a statement. Of course, the spouse exemption will never apply if the employer is a company, irrespective of the relationship of the employee and any director or shareholder of the company, with whom the employee deals.

If any change is made in the matters referred to in the written statement, there is a special procedure for notifying the change to an employee. Legal advice should always be taken.

Most employees will also be entitled to an itemised statement of pay, containing necessary information as to, for example, the gross and net pay, and the amount and nature of any deductions made.

The employer does not automatically have to provide the employee with work, provided that the employee is being given the benefits which the employer agreed to give in the contract of employment. An employee may therefore be given work as and when the employer wishes. However, there may be tax problems if the benefits being given to the employee are out of proportion to work being done.

Health and safety at work are important matters, and the employer must be sure that the legal and other requirements are observed at work premises. There are a number of Acts of Parliament which may apply, dealing with matters as diverse as cleanliness of machinery, and use of lifting tackle. However, the basic duty behind all the legislation and rules is the duty requiring the employer to take reasonable care for the safety of employees. This duty is commonly divided into three limbs, whereby the employer must provide:

(1)   competent staff;
(2)   adequate machinery, plant, premises and materials;
(3)   proper systems of work and supervision.

What this entails will depend upon the nature of the business carried on by the employer, and the particular job of the employee. The employer should ensure that proper advice is taken in respect of its own particular business.

Discrimination is also proscribed by legislation. Discrimination may occur because of sex, race, nationality, colour, ethnic or national origins, marital status, previous criminal offences committed by the employee, trade union membership, or through unfair selection for dismissal or redundancy. Quite apart from existing employees, the question of possible discrimination should be carefully considered when advertising for new employees, or for employees to fill new positions. Discriminatory advertising is unlawful for both the employer and the publication where the advertisement appears.

The employer is responsible for paying contributions to social security, both on its own account, and on behalf of the employee. The employer must also insure all employees against liability for bodily injury and disease suffered in the course of, or because of, their employment. Other types of insurance which the employer should consider include the following:

(1)   public and product liability insurance;
(2)   fire and special perils;
(3)   theft cover;
(4)   business interruption insurance;
(5)   glass insurance;
(6)   money insurance and credit insurance;
(7)   documents and goods in transit;
(8)   motor insurance;
(9)   business travel insurance;
(10) professional indemnity;
(11) engineering insurance;
(12) personal accident insurance;
(13) personal health insurance;
(14) directors' and officers' liability insurance.

It is possible to get single policy insurance for particular trades, so that only one premium need be paid to cover an amalgamation of appropriate policies.

There is a complex body of law governing the rights of employees in relation to sickness, pregnancy, dismissal and redundancy. The employer must have a proper understanding of the principles behind this body of law. Legal advice should always be sought in specific cases. However, a further consideration of the detailed rules is beyond the scope of this book.

List of minority rights of shareholders

There follows below a list of the rights of minority shareholders.

Description of right	*Description of the type and minimum size of group required to exercise right*
Any shareholder can petition the court and show that the company's affairs are being or have been conducted in a manner which is unfairly prejudicial to the interests of some part of the shareholders (including himself) or to all of them or that an act or proposed act or omission of the company is or would be prejudicial. The court has very wide discretion to make whatever order it thinks fit.	*Any* shareholder of the company.
To apply to the court for the company to be wound up on the grounds that it is 'just and equitable' that the company should be wound up. Note that the application should show that the person applying has an interest in the winding up, ie there will be some surplus assets to be distributed. Because a successful application 'kills' the company it will usually be in a shareholder's interests to use another right if one is available.	*Any* shareholder of the company.
In the case of a company which has passed an elective resolution to dispense with the obligation to appoint auditors, to propose that the appointment of the company's auditors be brought to an end. This right must be exercised by depositing a notice in writing at the registered office. Only one such notice may be deposited by any one shareholder in any financial year.	*Any* shareholder of the company.
In the case of a company which has passed an elective resolution to dispense with the holding of annual general meetings, to require that such a meeting be held in a particular year. This right must be exercised not later than three months before the end of the year by notice to the company.	Any shareholder of the company.
In the case of a company which has passed an elective resolution to dispense with the laying of accounts and reports before the company in general meeting, to require that a general meeting be held for the purpose of laying a particular set of accounts and reports before the company. This right must be exercised within 28 days beginning with the day the relevant accounts and reports are	*Any* shareholder of the company.

Description of right	*Description of the type and minimum size of group required to exercise right*
sent out, by depositing a notice in writing at the registered office.	
To apply to the court for an order restraining the company from carrying out a future 'ultra vires' act, ie an act which it has no legal power to do because it is not authorised by its memorandum.	A minority shareholder.
To apply to the court on behalf of all innocent shareholders for compensation in respect of an act which is not authorised by the company's memorandum of association but which has already been committed. Note there are very strict legal rules which must be satisfied before such an action can succeed, for example there must have been a fraud on the minority and the wrongdoers must be in control of the company.	A minority shareholder.
To apply to the court for relief where his personal rights as a shareholder have been infringed. Note it is very difficult to provide any useful guidance as to when the courts will allow such an application to succeed. There must have been a very fundamental type of wrong done to the applicant which cannot be ratified by the majority of shareholders – for example, an attempt to remove the applicant's right to vote. It is therefore not advisable to rely on this right unless no other remedies are available. It is only likely to be successful in *extreme* circumstances.	*Any* shareholder of the company.
To requisition the holding of an extraordinary general meeting, notwithstanding anything in the articles of the company.	Holders of one-tenth of the paid-up capital carrying voting rights at the date of the deposit of the requisition.
In the case of a company otherwise entitled to an exemption from the audit requirement, or to replace it with a compilation report, to require the company to comply with the full statutory audit requirement. This right must be exercised by notice in writing deposited at the registered office not later than one month before the end of the financial year to which the relevant accounts relate.	Holders of 10% of the issued capital of the company or of any class.

Description of right	Description of the type and minimum size of group required to exercise right
To apply to the court for cancellation of an alteration to conditions in memorandum which could have been contained in articles. The court has wide powers to make such an order as it thinks fit.	Holders of 15% of the issued capital of the company or of any class.
To apply to the court for cancellation of variation of class rights: (i) where the memorandum or articles provide for such variations to be subject to the consent of a specified proportion of that class or a resolution of that class; (ii) where class rights not contained in the memorandum and the articles do not contain provisions for the variation of class rights.	Holders of 15% of the issued shares of the relevant class, being persons who did not consent to or vote in favour of the variation.
To requisition the circulation of resolutions and notices. Resolutions of which notice is given in this way are to be dealt with at an AGM, notwithstanding anything in the articles.	(i) Shareholders representing one-twentieth of the total voting rights of all the shareholders having a right to vote at the meeting to which the requisition relates; or (ii) not less than 100 shareholders holding shares on which there has been paid up an average sum of at least £100 per shareholder.
To demand a poll at a general meeting on any question other than the election of the chairman of the meeting or the adjournment of the meeting. Any provision in the articles preventing this is void.	(i) Five shareholders having the right to vote at the relevant meeting; or (ii) a shareholder or shareholders representing one-tenth of the total voting rights of all shareholders having the right to vote at that meeting; or (iii) a shareholder or shareholders holding shares in the company conferring a right to vote at the meeting and upon which has been paid up at least one-tenth of the total sum paid up on all shares carrying that right.

Description of right	Description of the type and minimum size of group required to exercise right
To apply to the court for cancellation of a special resolution approving any payment out of capital for the redemption or purchase by a private company of its shares. Application must be made within 5 weeks of the date on which the resolution was passed.	Any member of the company other than one who consented to or voted in favour of the resolution (any creditor of the company may also apply).

List of matters to be dealt with by shareholders under the Companies Acts – brief information

Alteration of objects

A company may alter its memorandum with regard to its objects by passing a special resolution.

Alteration of articles

Subject to the provisions of the Companies Acts and to the conditions contained in its memorandum, a company may alter its articles by passing a special resolution.

Change of name

A company may change its name by passing a special resolution. Note the change does not take effect until the registrar of companies issues a certificate of incorporation on change of name.

Alterations to capital

If authorised by its articles a company may, by ordinary resolution passed in general meeting:

(1) increase its share capital by creating new shares;
(2) consolidate and divide all or any of its share capital into shares of larger amount than its existing shares;
(3) convert all or any of its paid-up shares into stock and reconvert that stock into paid-up shares of any denomination;
(4) subdivide any of its shares into shares of a smaller amount;
(5) cancel shares not issued at the date of the passing of the resolution to cancel them and thereby diminish its share capital by that amount.

Shares are subdivided if, for example, one share of £1 is turned into ten shares of 10p. Shares are consolidated if, for example, five shares of £1 each are turned into one share of £5. When consolidating shares in this way, care must be taken to ensure that each shareholder will end up with a whole number of shares.

Reduction of capital

A company may pass a special resolution to reduce its capital – an application to the court for an order to confirm the reduction must then be made. There are various detailed and complex procedures laid down in the Companies Acts in connection with a reduction of capital, especially concerning publicity for the proposal.

Alteration of a condition in a memorandum which could have been in the articles

Such a condition may be altered by special resolution although the court has power to cancel the alteration.

Annual general meeting

An annual general meeting of every company must be held in every calendar year and not more than 15 months must elapse between one annual general meeting and the next. This does not apply if the members of the company have passed a valid 'elective resolution'.

Declaration of dividends

Subject to the provisions of its own articles, a company usually declares dividends after the end of an accounting reference period by passing a resolution in general meeting. However, the articles often allow the directors of the company to pay an 'interim' dividend during the course of an accounting reference period without referring the matter to the shareholders.

Giving authority to the directors to allot shares

The directors of a company cannot allot any shares unless they have been given authority to do so either by the company's articles or by ordinary resolution passed in general meeting.

Removal of a director

A company may, by ordinary resolution of which special notice has been given, remove a director at any time regardless of anything in its articles or in any agreement between it and the director.

At least 28 days before the meeting at which such a resolution is to be proposed, special notice of the resolution must be given to the company by the shareholder(s) proposing it and the company must then give at least 21 days' notice of the meeting to all its shareholders.

A director should not be removed unless professional advice has been taken.

Authorising the giving of financial assistance

Generally, a company is prohibited from giving financial assistance to a third party for the purpose of an acquisition of the company's shares but in some circumstances it may do so. If the proposed financial assistance is authorised by the Act the giving of it must be approved in advance by special resolution of the company. Note that there are other essential detailed procedural requirements which must be observed to make the giving of the financial assistance lawful.

Authorising a purchase by the company of its own shares

In certain circumstances, a company can purchase its own shares.

If a private or public company is proposing to do so and the purchase money is to come from its distributable profits then the contract for the purchase must be given prior approval by a special resolution of the company.

If a private company is proposing to do so and the purchase money is to come from capital that payment out of capital must be approved by a special resolution of the company. (Note that if the proposed payment is to be made from capital the company's creditors or any dissenting shareholder can apply to the court for cancellation of the special resolution. Note also that there are complex procedural requirements in respect of a purchase of a company's own shares which must be observed – the requirements are particularly stringent in the case of a purchase from capital.)

Appointment of auditors (if required)

At each general meeting of the company at which accounts are laid, every company must appoint auditors to hold office from that general meeting to the next general meeting at which accounts are laid. This does not apply if the members of the company have passed a valid 'elective resolution'.

Fixing of auditors' remuneration

Auditors' remuneration is fixed or the manner of determining remuneration is fixed by resolution of the company in general meeting.

Removal of auditors

A company may remove its auditor before the expiration of the auditor's term of office, regardless of anything in any agreement between the auditor and the company, by passing an ordinary resolution of which special notice has been given.

Exempting the company from the obligation to appoint auditors

A company can exempt itself completely from the obligation to appoint auditors by passing a special resolution in general meeting, but only if it is a 'dormant' company, or does not need to appoint auditors under the current small company exemptions.

Director's contract of employment for more than 5 years

Where it is proposed that a provision should be included in an agreement whereby a director's employment is to continue (or may continue) for a period of more than 5 years and during that time the employment:

(1)   cannot be terminated by the company by notice; or
(2)   can be terminated only in specified circumstances,

then that provision must have the prior approval of the company given by a resolution passed in general meeting.

Substantial property transactions involving directors

The prior approval of the shareholders must be given by a resolution in general meeting before a company enters an agreement:

(1)   whereby a director or a person connected with a director, acquires or is to acquire one or more non-cash assets of a specified value; or
(2)   whereby the company acquires or is to acquire one or more non-cash assets of a specified value from a director or a person connected with a director.

Professional advice will be required with regard to the 'specified value' and note that there are some exceptions to this rule.

Shareholders' voluntary winding up

If a company is solvent, its shareholders can pass a special resolution that the company should be wound up. During the course of the winding-up there will be periodic meetings of the company's shareholders and eventually there will be a final general meeting.

Voluntary arrangement under the insolvency legislation of 1986

A liquidator, administrator or the directors of a company may propose a composition in satisfaction of the company's debts or a scheme of arrangement of its affairs which is to be implemented under the supervision of a qualified insolvency practitioner. That qualified insolvency practitioner may summon meetings of the shareholders to consider the proposal and to approve or modify or reject it.

Application for re-registration of a private company as a public company

A private company may apply to the registrar of companies for re-registration as a public company. Before making such an application the shareholders must pass a special resolution that the company should be so re-registered, and comply with other detailed procedural requirements.

Application for re-registration of a limited company as an unlimited company

A private company registered as a limited company can apply to the registrar of companies for re-registration as an unlimited company. Every shareholder must sign a statutory 'Form of Assent', agreeing to the company being so re-registered.

Note: this is not an exhaustive list.

Company searches and trade mark searches *

Company searches

It is a simple and quick matter, on payment of a fee, to find out information about companies appearing on the companies index of England and Wales, Scotland or Northern Ireland, by making a company search at the appropriate Companies House, or any branch of it. Such a search may be carried out personally, or through a lawyer, accountant or company search agent.

It is also possible to access data, or electronic images of documents filed, through various on-line services. Web-based services include Companies House Direct, available via www.companieshouse.gov.uk or JordanWatch, at www.jordans.co.uk.

When making a search, it is crucial that the company name given to Companies House, or to a search agent, is absolutely correct. For example, the names of companies referred to in the financial press are often not the true corporate names of the companies referred to. If the wrong name is given the search will be rejected, or a search may even be made against a company with a similar name, and a fee charged accordingly.

To avoid problems with the name, the company number should, if possible, always be given. A company may have changed its name but it cannot change its company number. Cross-checking of the two should reduce search errors.

The public file of a company at Companies House contains documents which have been filed by, or notices which have been entered against, the company. Such information is either notified to the registrar on official forms, or in a particular format. All company records are therefore consistent, and information is easy to find. Companies House record all such information on microfiche and in their computer. Companies House also has similar records for companies incorporated outside Great Britain or Northern Ireland which have established a place of business or a branch in Great Britain or Northern Ireland. All companies will submit information in three broad classifications:

(1) General information relating to the constitution and management of a company. This includes the original registration documents of the company and the certificate of incorporation. In the case of a public limited company, the register will further show a trading certificate. It also includes all resolutions or orders effecting an alteration to the memorandum and articles of association, together with copies of the memorandum and articles of association as altered from time to time, any change in the structure of the authorised and issued share capital of the company, any changes in the registered office and officers of the company, any removal or resignation of the auditors and the appointment of a liquidator.
(2) Financial information relating to a company. This includes the annual accounts of the company and the annual returns as required by the Acts.
(3) Information relating to the registrable charges of a company. This includes the details of charges of the company, including, where applicable, notice of the appointment of a receiver or liquidator.

The public register of an overseas company, as mentioned above, will contain details of the constitution and officers of the company and other details required by the Act.

There is invariably a delay between delivery of documents for registration and their appearance on the public record. However, the registrar of companies will alert the searcher to the existence of certain important documents received but not filmed, by including a 'flag' in the company records. These documents include charges and liquidation documents.

Since the companies index is now computerised, it is possible to ask a company search agent to 'monitor' the companies index daily, to ensure that, in the event that any new companies are formed with a name similar to an existing company name or business name, this is reported to the owners of the existing name. This allows objections to the Secretary of State for Trade and Industry, or passing-off actions, to be instituted quickly and effectively against the new company.

Trade mark searches **

Trade marks are a means of identification. They are a symbol (whether a word or device, or a combination of the two) which a sole trader, partnership or company uses in the course of trade, or business, in order that his goods or services may be readily distinguished by the public from similar goods or services provided by others. The statutory definition is 'any sign capable of being represented graphically … including the shape of goods or of their packaging …'.

A trade mark must be distinctive. For example, in the case of a trade mark for goods, it must be independent of the 'design' of the goods, and of any descriptive wording or purely decorative matter with which it may be associated in ordinary use. For example, no protection will be conferred upon the trader who describes his products as 'good blue butterfly-shaped birthday cards' under the trade marks law. These words are not distinctive, but descriptive words, in ordinary use. In the case of a trade mark for services, it must be different from any word, device, or combination of the two, that others may wish to use in the normal course of their business in relation to the same service.

It used to be the case that it was almost impossible to register geographical or personal names, but these strict rules have been relaxed considerably.

The registration of trade marks is governed by the trade marks legislation. It is quite possible to own a trade mark which is not registered under this legislation through rights acquired by usage of the mark, in which case the mark may be protected by a 'passing-off' action in the courts if another trader uses a mark which is identical or similar to an existing mark. However, registration confers additional protections on the owner.

Registration and search are effected at the Patent Office in Newport, Gwent which covers the entire UK.

Goods and services are internationally classified into 42 classes. A mark will be registered against one or more classes of goods or service, *and will protect the mark only in respect of classes in which it is registered*. The registrar of trade marks is, quite rightly, very fussy as to the precise class or classes into which a particular product or service falls. It is possible to apply for registration across a range of classes in only one application.

Official registration of a mark is undertaken by the Patent Office and Trade Marks Registry and any searching against a trade mark is carried out there. Once registered, the mark must be renewed every 10 years.

On payment of a fee, anyone may search amongst the representations and indices of trade marks for goods and services in all classes at the trade marks branch of the Patent Office.

The indices include a classified index of devices and drawings/logos, and alphabetical indices of words occurring as trade marks or parts of trade marks. These are arranged according to their beginnings and endings. The indices include pending applications for registration as well as those marks already protected by registration.

Hearing officers are available for consultation, by appointment, to provide assistance on interpreting search results, among other things, and helping to explore ways of amending a proposed mark to distinguish it from similar marks found during a search. This service is not available for the discussion of marks that are already subject to an application for registration.

Searches of the trade marks register and applications for registration of a trade mark may be made by any member of the public, though it is always prudent to use agents in light of their expertise and knowledge of trade mark law. A search will ensure that a proposed mark, or a mark similar to it, is not already being used by some other person.

It is also possible to register trade marks in other jurisdictions and/or at certain international registers which confer protections in a number of jurisdictions. Searches may also be made in these other jurisdictions or at the international registers. Again, an adviser should be consulted if a registration or search may be required in these other registers.

Stationery and premises *

Business documents

A company carrying on a business must give particular details on certain of its business documents:

ITS NAME Every company must state its name, exactly as it appears on its certificate of incorporation or any certificate on change of name, on all its business letters and on other official documents. These include all its 'notices and other official publications', all 'bills of exchange, promissory notes, endorsements, cheques and orders for money or goods purporting to be signed by or on behalf of the company, and in all its bills of parcel, invoices, receipts and letters of credit'.

ITS DESIGNATION The name includes, of course, the words 'Limited', 'Ltd', 'public limited company' or 'plc', or, where appropriate, their Welsh equivalent, and these must be included.

Where such words are included in their Welsh form, the fact that the company is a limited company, or a public limited company, must be stated in English in legible characters on all its prospectuses, bill heads, letter paper, notices and official publications.

Where dispensation has been obtained from the requirement to include the word 'Limited', the fact that the company is a limited company must be stated in legible characters on all its business letters and order forms.

ITS PLACE OF REGISTRATION, REGISTERED NUMBER AND ADDRESS OF REGISTERED OFFICE Every company must print its place of registration (such as 'England and Wales'), the number with which it is registered, and the address of its registered office, legibly, in all its business letters and order forms.

Even where only one address is shown, an indication should be given that this is the registered office of the company. For example, a statement at the foot of a page might say 'registered office as above'.

Whilst there is no requirement to state directors' names on business letters, if one director is named (other than in the text of the letter, or as a signatory) then all must be named.

A Christian name or an initial must be included, and, where another company holds office as a director of the company the company name of the corporate director must be given.

Whilst there is no requirement to state the share capital of a company on its business documents, if a company does so, it is the company's paid-up share capital which must be specified.

Business premises

ITS NAME A company must keep its name painted or affixed on the outside of every office or place in which its business is carried on, in a conspicuous position, and in legible form.

Where the name of a company or public company includes the equivalent in Welsh of the words 'Limited' or 'public limited company', such words must also be stated in English.

BUSINESS NAME In its registered office and in any premises where a business is carried on by a company and to which the customers or suppliers have access, the company must display, in a prominent position, a notice stating its name and registered office address.

Overseas companies

An overseas company which has established a place of business or a branch in Great Britain or Northern Ireland must state, legibly, its name, the country in which it is incorporated and, if the liability of the members of the company is limited, notice of that fact, in every prospectus inviting subscriptions for its shares or debentures in Great Britain or Northern Ireland, and on all bills, letterheads, notices and other official publications of the company in Great Britain or Northern Ireland.

An overseas company must also display, in any premises where a business is carried on by it, and to which the customers or suppliers have access, in a prominent position, a notice stating its name.

Leasing

The concept of a lease

It is increasingly difficult to describe accurately what a lease is, as the number of alternative packages available increases almost monthly.

Broadly speaking, a lease is the rental of an asset for a specified period of time. There may be an advance payment (ie deposit) required at the start of the lease, and there may also (or usually instead) be a lump sum due at the end of the period.

Different possibilities could be as follows.

EXAMPLE 1

Asset cost = £10,000

Leasing payment = 3 × £300 (ie £900) deposit plus 36 × £300

At the end of the period, the asset may be 'leased' for a nominal or peppercorn rent of, say, £5 pa.

In example 1, what has basically happened is that the lease (the party renting the use of the asset) has paid for the asset over the 3 years. He may continue to use the asset at the end of the period for a nominal amount per year. Depending on the actual agreement, he may be able to purchase the asset from the leasing company at the end of the period. The differences between this type of lease and a hire-purchase type of arrangement are few and subtle and may be summarised as:

(1) more advantageous cash flow for the lessee as hire-purchase will normally require a higher deposit, as a percentage of the cost price; and

(2) different tax treatment of the payments in the lessee's tax computation (see below).

Although the cash flow is slightly improved on this type of lease, the lessee will probably pay more out than in a hire-purchase agreement for the same asset over the same period, as more interest will be charged (as part of the leasing payment) on a lease, with the average amount borrowed being higher across the period of borrowing – the period of the lease.

EXAMPLE 2

Asset cost = £10,000

36 payments of £200 monthly plus lump sum

At end of period the asset would be sold and the lump sum paid off.

This is often termed a residual value lease.

This is basically the same as example 1, the only difference being that the lessee repays less of the cost of the asset (or amount borrowed). An assumption is made on the percentage by which the value of the asset will have fallen by the end of the lease period (ie the depreciation suffered), and some of the borrowing will be deferred and become payable at the end of the lease period.

For example, a car costing £20,000 may be assumed to depreciate by 50 per cent over the 3-year period. Building in a safety margin, the lessor will require the lessee to repay, say, £12,000 (50% × £20,000 plus £2,000 – the safety margin) over the 3 years plus interest on the whole £20,000.

Then after 3 years, the lease finishes, the car is sold for £9,000 and the lessee has a balance of £1,000 (£20,000 – £12,000 – £9,000) to use as a deposit on another vehicle. This method is very popular for the purchase of expensive motor cars, as they would be very expensive to buy on a straight hire-purchase or loan basis. The lessors do not object to the arrangement because they are lending money against assets which fairly reliably will depreciate at a known rate.

EXAMPLE 3
Asset cost = £1,000
Monthly rental of £25 for 4 years then returned to leasing company.

The third example would typically be a straight rental of an item such as a television or a photocopier. The lessee would not always wish to own the asset because the items may constantly be updated. A residual lease would not be suitable as the asset when secondhand would have a very low resale value.

Taxation treatment of leasing payments

The taxation treatment of leasing payments is a fairly complex subject and the amount of the payment which may be treated as a deduction from profits is a matter which should be confirmed with the leasing company before the document is signed.

Broadly speaking, for all items except private motor cars, all the leasing payments (except, of course, VAT, which will be reclaimed in the normal way) will be allowable as a deduction against profits.

For motor cars, there is a formula which calculates a restriction on the leasing payments which is currently as follows:

$$\text{Disallowed portion} = \text{leasing payments} \times \left[\left(\frac{\text{cost of car} - \pounds12{,}000}{2} \right) \div \text{cost of car} \right]$$

so for a car costing (and this refers to the original cost with a secondhand car) £20,000 and annual leasing payments of £4,800, the disallowed portion would be:

$$\pounds4{,}800 \times \left[\left(\frac{\pounds20{,}000 - \pounds12{,}000}{2} \right) \div 20{,}000 \right]$$

that is to say

$$\pounds4{,}800 \times 20\% = \pounds960$$

As can be seen from the example, the original cost of the car can have a significant effect on the allowability of the leasing payments, and therefore the real cost to the company of running that type of car.

As if this is not complicated enough, only 50 per cent of the VAT paid on car leasing payments can be reclaimed.

APPENDIX A

Useful Addresses

ACAS

Brandon House
180 Borough High Street
London SE1 1LW
Tel: 020 7396 5100

Franborough House
123/157 Bothwell Street
Glasgow G2 7JR
Tel: 0141 204 2677

3 Purbeck House
Lambourne Crescent
Llanishen
Cardiff CF14 5GJ
Tel: 029 2076 1126
www.acas.org.uk

Advertising Standards Authority

2 Torrington Place
London WC1E 7HW
Tel: 020 7580 5555
www.asa.org.uk

Association of Chartered Certified Accountants

29 Lincoln's Inn Fields
London WC2A 3EE
Tel: 020 7396 5800
www.accaglobal.com

The British Chambers of Commerce

Manning House
22 Carlisle Place
London SW1P 1JA
Tel: 020 7565 2000
www.britishchambers.org.uk

British Franchise Association

Thames View
Newtown Road
Henley-on-Thames RG9 1HG
Tel: 01491 578050
www.british-franchise.org

Chartered Institute of Arbitrators

12 Bloomsbury Square
London WC1A 2LP
Tel: 020 7404 4023
www.arbitrators.org

Citizens Advice Bureaux

(see under Citizens Advice Bureaux in your local telephone directory)
www.nacab.org.uk

Commission for Racial Equality

Elliot House
10/12 Allington Street
London SW1E 5EH
Tel: 020 7828 7022

Hanover House
45–51 Hanover Street
Edinburgh EH2 2PJ
Tel: 0131 240 2600

14th Floor
Capital Tower
Greyfriars Road
Cardiff CF1 3AG
Tel: 02920 388977
www.cre.gov.uk

Companies House

Crown Way
Cardiff CF4 3UZ
Tel: 0870 333 3636

37 Castle Terrace
Edinburgh EH1 2EB
Tel: 0870 333 3636
www.companieshouse.gov.uk

Consumer's Association

2 Marylebone Road
London NW1 4DF
Tel: 020 7830 6000
www.which.net

The Countryside Agency

John Dower House
Crescent Place
Cheltenham
Gloucestershire GL50 3RA
Tel: 01242 521381
www.countryside.gov.uk

Department of Social Security

(see Department for Work and
Pensions)

Department of Trade and Industry

Regional Development and Inward
Investment
Kingsgate House
66–74 Victoria Street
London SWIE 6SW
Tel: 020 7215 2578
www.dti.gov.uk

Department for Work and Pensions

(see under Work and Pensions
Department of, or Social Security
Department of, in your local
telephone directory)
Tel: 0800 393539 (freephone helpline)

Enterprise Grants

Business Link Signpost
Tel: 0845 600 9006
www.dti.gov.uk/enterprisegrant

Equal Opportunities Commission

Arndale House
Arndale Centre
Manchester M4 3EQ
Tel: 0161 833 9244

Windsor House
Windsor Lane
Cardiff CF10 3GE
Tel: 029 2034 3552

St Stephens House
279 Bath Street
Glasgow G2 4JL
Tel: 0141 248 5833
www.eoc.gov.uk

Financial Ombudsman Service

South Quay Plaza
183 Marsh Wall
London E14 9SR
Tel: 0845 080 1800
www.financial-ombudsman.org.uk

Health and Safety Executive

HSE Infoline
Tel: 08701 545500
www.hse.gov.uk

Information Commissioner's Office

Wycliffe House
Water Lane
Wilmslow
Cheshire SK9 5AF
Tel: 01625 545 700
www.dataprotection.gov.uk

Inland Revenue

(see under Inland Revenue in your local
telephone directory)

The Insolvency Practitioners Association

Bow Bells House
11 Bread Street
London EC4M 9BE
Tel: 020 7329 0777

Institute of Chartered Accountants in England and Wales

Chartered Accountants Hall
Moorgate Place
London EC2P 2BJ
Tel: 020 7920 8100
www.icaew.co.uk

Institute of Chartered Accountants of Scotland

CA House
21 Haymarket Yards
Edinburgh EH12 5BH
Tel: 0131 347 0100
www.icas.org.uk

The Law Society of England and Wales

113 Chancery Lane
London WC2A 1PL
Tel: 020 7242 1222
www.lawsociety.org.uk

The Law Society of Northern Ireland

Law Society House
98 Victoria Street
Belfast BT1 3JZ
Tel: 02890 231614
www.lawsoc-ni.org

The Law Society of Scotland

26 Drumsheugh Gardens
Edinburgh EH3 7YR
Tel: 0131 226 7411
www.lawscot.org.uk

Local Authority Environmental Health Departments

(see under Local Authority in your local telephone directory)

Local Trading Standards Department

(see under Trading Standards in your local telephone directory)

London Enterprise Agency (also known as One London)

28 Park Street
London SE1 4EQ
Tel: 020 7248 5555
www.one-london.com

Office of Fair Trading

Fleetbank House
2–6 Salisbury Square
London EC4Y 8JX
Tel: 020 7211 8000
www.oft.gov.uk

The Patent Office

Concept House
Cardiff Road
Newport
Gwent NP10 8QQ
Tel: 08459 500 505
www.patent.gov.uk

Small Firms Advice Bureau

(dial 100 and ask for Freephone Enterprise)

Society of Practitioners of Insolvency

Halton House
20–23 Holborn
London EC1N 2JE
Tel: 020 7831 6563
www.insolvency.co.uk

The Registrar of Companies

Department of Economic Development
IDB House
64 Chichester Street
Belfast BT1 4JX
Tel: 02890 234488
www.companiesregistry-ni.gov.uk

VAT

(see under HM Customs & Excise in
your local telephone directory)

Welsh Development Agency

QED Centre
Main Avenue
Treforest
Mid Glamorgan CF37 5YR
Tel: 01433 845500
www.wda.co.uk

APPENDIX B

Sensitive Words and Expressions

Great Britain

You will need the approval of the Secretary of State for Trade and Industry before you use any of the following words or expressions (or their plural or possessive forms) in your chosen company name.

(a)   Words which imply national or international pre-eminence:

British	Great Britain	National	Wales
England	International	Scotland	Welsh
English	Ireland	Scottish	
European	Irish	United Kingdom	

(b)   Words which imply business pre-eminence or representative or authoritative status:

Association	Board	Federation	Institution
Authority	Council	Institute	Society

(c)   Words which imply specific objects or functions:

Assurance	Foundation	Patent	Sheffield
Assurer	Friendly society	Patentee	Stock exchange
Benevolent	Fund	Post office	Trade union
Charter	Group	Reassurance	Trust
Chartered	Holding	Reassurer	
Charity	Industrial &	Register	
Chemist	provident society	Registered	
Chemistry	Insurance	Reinsurance	
Co-operative	Insurer	Reinsurer	

Words or expressions in the following list need the approval of the Secretary of State. If you want to use any of them in your company name you will need to write first to the relevant body to ask if they have any objection to its use. When you apply for approval to use the name you should tell Companies House that you have written to the relevant body and enclose a copy of the reply you have received.

Word or Expression	Relevant Body for companies intending to have registered office in England or Wales	Relevant Body for companies intending to have registered office in Scotland
Apothecary	The Worshipful Society of Apothecaries of London Apothecaries Hall Blackfriars Lane London EC4V 6EJ	The Royal Pharmaceutical Society of Great Britain Law Department 1 Lambeth High Street London SEl 7JN
Charity Charitable	Charity Commission Registration Division Harmsworth House 13–15 Bouverie Street London EC4Y 8DP *or for companies **not** intending to register as a charity* Charity Commission 2nd Floor 20 Kings Parade Queens Dock Liverpool L3 4DQ	For recognition as a Scottish charity Inland Revenue FICO (Scotland) Trinity Park House South Trinity Road Edinburgh EH5 3SD
Contact Lens	The Registrar General Optical Council 41 Harley Street London W1N 2DJ	As for England and Wales
Dental Dentistry	The Registrar General Dental Council 37 Wimpole Street London W1M 8DQ	As for England and Wales
District Nurse Health Visitor Midwife Midwifery Nurse Nursing	The Registrar & Chief Executive United Kingdom Central Council for Nursing, Midwifery and Health Visiting 23 Portland Place London W1N 3AF	As for England and Wales
Health Centre	Office of the Solicitor Department of Health & Social Security 48 Carey Street London WC2A 2LS	As for England and Wales

Word or Expression	Relevant Body for companies intending to have registered office in England or Wales	Relevant Body for companies intending to have registered office in Scotland
Health Service	NHS Management Executive Department of Health Wellington House 133–155 Waterloo Road London SE1 8UG	As for England and Wales
Police	Home Office Police Dept Strategy Group Room 510 50 Queen Anne's Gate London SW1H 9AT	The Scottish Ministers Police Division St Andrews House Regent Road Edinburgh EH1 3DG
Polytechnic	Department for Education and Skills FHE 1B Sanctuary Buildings Great Smith Street Westminster London SW1P 3BT	As for England and Wales
Pregnancy Termination Abortion	Department of Health Area 423 Wellington House 133–135 Waterloo Road London SE1 8UG	As for England and Wales
Royal Royale Royalty King Queen Prince Princess Windsor Duke His/Her Majesty	*(If based in England)* Home Office A Division Room 730 50 Queen Anne's Gate London SW1H 9AT *(If based in Wales)* The National Assembly for Wales Crown Buildings Cathays Park Cardiff CF10 3NQ	The Scottish Ministers Civil Law and Legal Aid Division Saughton House Broomhouse Drive Edinburgh EH11 3XD
Special School	Department for Education and Skills Schools 2 Branch Sanctuary Buildings Great Smith Street Westminster London SW1P 3BT	As for England and Wales

Word or Expression	Relevant Body for companies intending to have registered office in England or Wales	Relevant Body for companies intending to have registered office in Scotland
University	Privy Council Office 68 Whitehall London SW1A 2AT	As for England and Wales

Certain words or expressions are covered by other legislation and their use in company names might be a criminal offence. These are listed below. If you want to use any of these words or expressions in your company name, then you should contact the relevant regulatory authority or ask Companies House for advice before proceeding. Companies House may seek independent advice from the relevant body.

Word or Expression	Relevant Legislation	Relevant Body
Anzac	Anzac Act 1916, s 1	Seek advice of Companies House
Architect	Architects Registration Act 1997, s 20	Architects Registration Board 73 Hallam Street London W1N 6EE
Bank Banker Banking Deposit	Banking Act 1987	Authorisation Enquiries Financial Services Authority 25 The North Colonnade Canary Wharf London E14 5HS
Building Society	Building Society Act 1986	Seek advice of Building Societies Commission Victoria House 30–40 Kingsway London WC2B 6ES

Word or Expression	Relevant Legislation	Relevant Body
Chamber(s) of Business Chamber(s) of Commerce Chamber(s) of Commerce and Industry Chamber(s) of Commerce, Training and Enterprise Chamber(s) of Enterprise Chamber(s) of Industry Chamber(s) of Trade Chamber(s) of Trade and Industry Chamber(s) of Training Chamber(s) of Training and Enterprise *Or the welsh translations of these words*	Company and Business Names (Chamber of Commerce etc) Act 1999	Seek advice of Companies House
Chiropodist Dietician Medical Laboratory Technician Occupational Therapist Orthoptist Physiotherapist Radiographer Remedial Gymnast	Professions Supplementary to Medicine Act 1960 if preceded by Registered, State or Registered	Room 12.26 HAP4 Division Department of Health Hannibal House Elephant & Castle London SE1 6TE
Credit Union	Credit Union Act 1979	The Registrar of Friendly Societies 25 The North Colonnade Canary Wharf London E14 5HS *(for Scottish Registered Companies)* Assistant Registrar of Friendly Societies 58 Frederick Street Edinburgh EH2 1NB
Dentist Dental Surgeon Dental Practitioner	Dental Act 1984	The Registrar General Dental Council 37 Wimpole Street London W1M 8DQ

Word or Expression	Relevant Legislation	Relevant Body
Drug Druggist Pharmaceutical Pharmaceutist Pharmaceutical, Pharmacist Pharmacy	Medicines Act 1968, s 78	The Director of Legal Services The Royal Society of Great Britain 1 Lambeth High Street London SE1 7JN *(for Scottish Registered Companies)* The Pharmaceutical Society 36 York Place Edinburgh EH1 3HU
Institute of Laryngology Institute of Otology Institute of Urology Institute of Orthopaedics	University College London Act 1988	Seek advice of University College Gower Street London WC1E 6BT
Insurance Broker Assurance Broker Re-Insurance Broker Re-Assurance Broker	Insurance Brokers (Registration) Act 1977, ss 2, 3	Seek advice of The Insurance Brokers Registration Council Higham Business Centre Midland Road Higham Ferrers Northants
Olympiad Olympiads Olympian Olympians Olympic Olympics *or translation of these words*	Olympic Symbol etc (Protection) Act 1995* **Also protects Olympic symbols of five interlocking rings and motto 'Citius Altius Forius'*	British Olympic Association 1 Wandsworth Plain London SW18 1EH
Optician Ophthalmic Optician Dispensing Optician Enrolled Optician Registered Optician Optometrist	Opticians Act 1989	The Registrar General Optical Council 41 Harley Street London W1N 2DJ

Word or Expression	Relevant Legislation	Relevant Body
Patent Office, Patent Agent	Copyright, Designs and Patents Act 1988	IPCD Hazlitt House 45 Southampton Buildings London WC2A 1AR
Red Cross Geneva Cross Red Crescent Red Lion and Sun	Geneva Convention Act 1957	Seek advice of Companies House
Veterinary Surgeon Veterinary Vet	Veterinary Surgeons Act 1966, ss 19, 20	The Registrar Royal College of Veterinary Surgeons 62–64 Horseferry Rd London SW1P 2AF

Northern Ireland

The following words and expressions require the consent of the Department of Economic Development before their use will be allowed in a business name. The words fall into the following categories:

(a)   Words which imply national or international pre-eminence

British	Great Britain	National	Ulster
England	International	Northern Ireland	United Kingdom
English	Ireland	Scotland	Wales
European	Irish	Scottish	Welsh

(b)   Words which imply governmental patronage or sponsorship

Authority
Board
Council

(c)   Words which imply business pre-eminence or representative status

Association	Institute	Society
Federation	Institution	

(d)   Words which imply specific objects or functions

Assurance	Charter	Holding	Register
Assurer	Chartered	Industrial &	Registered
Benevolent	Chemist	Provident Society	Reinsurance
Chamber of	Chemistry	Insurance	Reinsurer
Industry	Co-operative	Insurer	Sheffield
Chamber of	Foundation	Patent	Stock
Trade	Friendly Society	Patentee	Exchange
Chamber of	Fund	Post Office	Trade Union
Commerce	Giro	Reassurance	Trust
Charity	Group	Reassurer	

Words or expressions in the following list also need the approval of the Department. If you want to use any of them in your company name you will need to write to the relevant body to ask whether they have any objection to your use of the word or expression in your company name. When you apply for approval to use the name you should tell the Department that you have written to the relevant body and enclose a copy of any reply you have received.

Word or Expression	Relevant Body
Bank Banker	Banking Supervision Division Bank of England Threadneedle Street London EC2R 8AM
Breed Breeder Breeding	Livestock Improvement and General Division Department of Agriculture Dundonald House Upper Newtownards Road Belfast BT3 3SF
Charity Charitable	Charities Branch Department of Finance and Personnel Room 113 Rosepark House Upper Newtownards Road Belfast BT4 3NR
Contact Lens	The Registrar General Optical Council 41 Harley Street London W1N 2DJ
Dentist Dentistry	The Registrar General Dental Council 37 Wimpole Street London W1N 8DQ

Word or Expression	Relevant Body
Health Centre Health Service Nursing Home Pregnancy Termination Abortion	The Office of the Chief Executive Room 3D Department of Health and Social Services Dundonald House Upper Newtownards Road Belfast BT4 3SF
Nurse Nursing Midwife Midwifery Health Visitor District Nurse	National Board for Nursing, Midwifery and Health Visiting for Northern Ireland RAC House Chichester Street Belfast BT1 4JE
Police	The Secretary Northern Ireland Office Stormont House Stormont Belfast BT4 3ST
Royal Royale Royalty King Queen Prince Princess Windsor Duke His/Her Majesty	E2 Division (Room 718) Home Office Queen Anne's Gate London SW1H 9AT
Special School	Co-ordination Branch Department of Education Rathgael House Balloo Road Bangor Co Down BT19 2PR

The use of certain words in a business name may contravene other legislation. Owners of businesses wishing to use any of these words in a business name should therefore seek confirmation from the relevant body listed below that the use of the word in a business name does not contravene the relevant legislation. However, it should be noted that the list is not exhaustive.

Word or Expression	Relevant Legislation	Relevant Body
Anzac	Anzac Act 1916, s 1	Seek advice of Companies Registry
Apothecary		Seek advice of Companies registry
Architect	Architects Registration Act 1938, s 1	The Registrar Architects Registration Council of the United Kingdom 73 Hallam Street London W1N 6EE
Chemist Chemistry Drug Drugist Pharmaceutical Pharmaceutist Pharmacist Pharmacy	Medicines Act 1968, s 78	Seek advice of Companies Registry
Credit Union	Industrial and Provident Societies Act (Northern Ireland) 1969	Seek advice of Companies Registry
Dentist Dental Surgeon Dental Practitioner	Dentist Act 1957, ss 38, 39	The Registrar General Dental Council 37 Wimpole Street London W1M 8DQ
Insurance Broker Assurance Broker Insurance Brokers Re-Insurance Broker Re-Assurance Broker	Insurance Brokers (Registration) Act 1977, ss 2, 3	Registration Council 15 St Helens Place London EC3A 6DS
Ophthalmic Optician Dispensing Optician Registered Optician	Opticians Act 1958, ss 4, 22	The Registrar General Optical Council 41 Harley Street London W1N 2DJ
Red Cross	Geneva Convention Act 1957	Seek advice of Companies Registry
Veterinary Surgeon	Veterinary Surgeons Act 1960, ss 19, 20	The Registrar Royal College of Veterinary Surgeons 32 Belgrave Square London SW1X 8QP

APPENDIX C

The Companies Act 1985, Table A

Regulations for Management of a Company Limited by Shares

Table A as prescribed by the Companies (Tables A to F) Regulations 1985 (SI 1985 No 805), amended by the Companies (Tables A to F) (Amendment) Regulations 1985 (SI 1985 No 1052), and the Companies Act 1985 (Electronic Communications) Order 2000 (SI 2000 No 3373).

The regulations of Table A to the Companies Act 1985 apply to the Company save insofar as they are not excluded or varied by its Articles of Association.

Interpretation

1   In these regulations –

'the Act' means the Companies Act 1985 including any statutory modification or re-enactment thereof for the time being in force.

'the articles' means the articles of the company.

'clear days' in relation to the period of a notice means that period excluding the day when the notice is given or deemed to be given and the day for which it is given or on which it is to take effect.

communication' means the same as in the Electronic Communications Act 2000,

'electronic communication' means the same as in the Electronic Communications Act 2000

'executed' includes any mode of execution.

'office' means the registered office of the company.

'the holder' in relation to shares means the member whose name is entered in the register of members as the holder of the shares.

'the seal' means the common seal of the company.

'secretary' means the secretary of the company or any other person appointed to perform the duties of the secretary of the company, including a joint, assistant or deputy secretary.

'the United Kingdom' means Great Britain and Northern Ireland.

Unless the context otherwise requires, words or expressions contained in these regulations bear the same meaning as in the Act but excluding any statutory modification thereof not in force when these regulations become binding on the company.

Share Capital

2   Subject to the provisions of the Act and without prejudice to any rights attached to any existing shares, any share may be issued with such rights or restrictions as the company may by ordinary resolution determine.

3   Subject to the provisions of the Act, shares may be issued which are to be redeemed or are to be liable to be redeemed at the option of the company or the holder on such terms and in such manner as may be provided by the articles.

4   The company may exercise the powers of paying commissions conferred by the Act. Subject to the provisions of the Act, any such commission may be satisfied by the payment of cash or by the allotment of fully or partly paid shares or partly in one way and partly in the other.

5   Except as required by law, no person shall be recognised by the company as holding any share upon any trust and (except as otherwise provided by the articles or by law) the company shall not be bound by or recognise any interest in any share except an absolute right to the entirety thereof in the holder.

Share Certificates

6   Every member, upon becoming the holder of any shares, shall be entitled without payment to one certificate for all the shares of each class held by him (and, upon transferring a part of his holding of shares of any class, to a certificate for the balance of such holding) or several certificates each for one or more of his shares upon payment for every certificate after the first of such reasonable sum as the directors may determine. Every certificate shall be sealed with the seal and shall specify the number, class and distinguishing numbers (if any) of the shares to which it relates and the amount or respective amounts paid up thereon. The company shall not be bound to issue more than one certificate for shares held jointly by several persons and delivery of a certificate to one joint holder shall be a sufficient delivery to all of them.

7   If a share certificate is defaced, worn-out, lost or destroyed, it may be renewed on such terms (if any) as to evidence and indemnity and payment of the expenses reasonably incurred by the company in investigating evidence as the directors may determine but otherwise free of charge, and (in the case of defacement or wearing-out) on delivery up of the old certificate.

Lien

8   The company shall have a first and paramount lien on every share (not being a fully paid share) for all moneys (whether presently payable or not) payable at a fixed time or called in respect of that share. The directors may at any time declare any share to be wholly or in part exempt from the provisions of this regulation. The company's lien on a share shall extend to any amount payable in respect of it.

9   The company may sell in such manner as the directors determine any shares on which the company has a lien if a sum in respect of which the lien exists is presently payable and is not paid within fourteen clear days after notice has been given to the holder of the share or to the person entitled to it in consequence of the

death or bankruptcy of the holder, demanding payment and stating that if the notice is not complied with the shares may be sold.

10   To give effect to a sale the directors may authorise some person to execute an instrument of transfer of the shares sold to, or in accordance with the directions of, the purchaser. The title of the transferee to the shares shall not be affected by any irregularity in or invalidity of the proceedings in reference to the sale.

11   The net proceeds of the sale, after payment of the costs, shall be applied in payment of so much of the sum for which the lien exists as is presently payable, and any residue shall (upon surrender to the company for cancellation of the certificate for the shares sold and subject to a like lien for any moneys not presently payable as existed upon the shares before the sale) be paid to the person entitled to the shares at the date of the sale.

Calls on Shares and Forfeiture

12   Subject to the terms of allotment, the directors may make calls upon the members in respect of any moneys unpaid on their shares (whether in respect of nominal value or premium) and each member shall (subject to receiving at least fourteen clear days' notice specifying when and where payment is to be made) pay to the company as required by the notice the amount called on his shares. A call may be required to be paid by instalments. A call may, before receipt by the company of any sum due thereunder, be revoked in whole or part and payment of a call may be postponed in whole or part. A person upon whom a call is made shall remain liable for calls made upon him notwithstanding the subsequent transfer of the shares in respect whereof the call was made.

13   A call shall be deemed to have been made at the time when the resolution of the directors authorising the call was passed.

14   The joint holders of a share shall be jointly and severally liable to pay all calls in respect thereof.

15   If a call remains unpaid after it has become due and payable the person from whom it is due and payable shall pay interest on the amount unpaid from the day it became due and payable until it is paid at the rate fixed by the terms of allotment of the share or in the notice of the call or, if no rate is fixed, at the appropriate rate (as defined by the Act) but the directors may waive payment of the interest wholly or in part.

16   An amount payable in respect of a share on allotment or at any fixed date, whether in respect of nominal value or premium or as an instalment of a call, shall be deemed to be a call and if it is not paid the provisions of the articles shall apply as if that amount had become due and payable by virtue of a call.

17   Subject to the terms of allotment, the directors may make arrangements on the issue of shares for a difference between the holders in the amounts and times of payment of calls on their shares.

18   If a call remains unpaid after it has become due and payable the directors may give to the person from whom it is due not less than fourteen clear days' notice requiring payment of the amount unpaid together with any interest which may have accrued. The notice shall name the place where payment is to be made and shall state that if the notice is not complied with the shares in respect of which the call was made will be liable to be forfeited.

19   If the notice is not complied with any share in respect of which it was given

may, before the payment required by the notice has been made, be forfeited by a resolution of the directors and the forfeiture shall include all dividends or other moneys payable in respect of the forfeited shares and not paid before the forfeiture.

20   Subject to the provisions of the Act, a forfeited share may be sold, re-allotted or otherwise disposed of on such terms and in such manner as the directors determine either to the person who was before the forfeiture the holder or to any other person and at any time before sale, re-allotment or other disposition, the forfeiture may be cancelled on such terms as the directors think fit. Where for the purposes of its disposal a forfeited share is to be transferred to any person the directors may authorise some person to execute an instrument of transfer of the share to that person.

21   A person any of whose shares have been forfeited shall cease to be a member in respect of them and shall surrender to the company for cancellation the certificate for the shares forfeited but shall remain liable to the company for all moneys which at the date of forfeiture were presently payable by him to the company in respect of those shares with interest at the rate at which interest was payable on those moneys before the forfeiture or, if no interest was so payable, at the appropriate rate (as defined in the Act) from the date of forfeiture until payment but the directors may waive payment wholly or in part or enforce payment without any allowance for the value of the shares at the time of forfeiture or for any consideration received on their disposal.

22   A statutory declaration by a director or the secretary that a share has been forfeited on a specified date shall be conclusive evidence of the facts stated in it as against all persons claiming to be entitled to the share and the declaration shall (subject to the execution of an instrument of transfer if necessary) constitute a good title to the share and the person to whom the share is disposed of shall not be bound to see to the application of the consideration, if any, nor shall his title to the share be affected by any irregularity in or invalidity of the proceedings in reference to the forfeiture or disposal of the share.

Transfer of Shares

23   The instrument of transfer of a share may be in any usual form or in any other form which the directors may approve and shall be executed by or on behalf of the transferor and, unless the share is fully paid, by or on behalf of the transferee.

24   The directors may refuse to register the transfer of a share which is not fully paid to a person of whom they do not approve and they may refuse to register the transfer of a share on which the company has a lien. They may also refuse to register a transfer unless:

> (a) it is lodged at the office or at such other places as the directors may appoint and is accompanied by the certificate for the shares to which it relates and such other evidence as the directors may reasonably require to show the right of the transferor to make the transfer;
> (b) it is in respect of only one class of shares; and
> (c) it is in favour of not more than four transferees.

25   If the directors refuse to register a transfer of a share, they shall within two months after the date on which the transfer was lodged with the company send to the transferee notice of the refusal.

26   The registration of transfers of shares or of transfers of any class of shares may

be suspended at such times and for such periods (not exceeding thirty days in any year) as the directors may determine.

27　No fee shall be charged for the registration of any instrument of transfer or other document relating to or affecting the title to any share.

28　The company shall be entitled to retain any instrument of transfer which is registered, but any instrument of transfer which the directors refuse to register shall be returned to the person lodging it when notice of the refusal is given.

Transmission of Shares

29　If a member dies the survivor or survivors where he was a joint holder, and his personal representatives where he was a sole holder or the only survivor of joint holders, shall be the only persons recognised by the company as having any title to his interest; but nothing herein contained shall release the estate of a deceased member from any liability in respect of any share which had been jointly held by him.

30　A person becoming entitled to a share in consequence of the death or bankruptcy of a member may, upon such evidence being produced as the directors may properly require, elect either to become the holder of the share or to have some person nominated by him registered as the transferee. If he elects to become the holder he shall give notice to the company to that effect. If he elects to have another person registered he shall execute an instrument of transfer of the share to that person. All the articles relating to the transfer of shares shall apply to the notice or instrument of transfer as if it were an instrument of transfer executed by the member and the death or bankruptcy of the member had not occurred.

31　A person becoming entitled to a share in consequence of the death or bankruptcy of a member shall have the rights to which he would be entitled if he were the holder of the share, except that he shall not, before being registered as the holder of the share, be entitled in respect of it to attend or vote at any meeting of the company or at any separate meeting of the holders of any class of shares in the company.

Alteration of Share Capital

32　The company may by ordinary resolution –

(a) increase its share capital by new shares of such amount as the resolution prescribes;
(b) consolidate and divide all or any of its share capital into shares of larger amount than its existing shares;
(c) subject to the provisions of the Act, sub-divide its shares, or any of them, into shares of smaller amount and the resolution may determine that, as between the shares resulting from the sub-division, any of them may have any preference or advantage as compared with the others; and
(d) cancel shares which, at the date of the passing of the resolution, have not been taken or agreed to be taken by any person and diminish the amount of its share capital by the amount of the shares so cancelled.

33　Whenever as a result of a consolidation of shares any members would become entitled to fractions of a share, the directors may, on behalf of those members, sell the shares representing the fractions for the best price reasonably obtainable to any person (including, subject to the provisions of the Act, the company) and distribute the net proceeds of sale in due proportion among those members, and the directors may authorise some person to execute an instrument of transfer of the shares to, or in accordance with the directions of, the purchaser. The transferee shall not be bound to see to the application of the purchase money nor shall his title to the shares be affected by any irregularity in or invalidity of the proceedings in reference to the sale.

34   Subject to the provisions of the Act, the company may by special resolution reduce its share capital, any capital redemption reserve and any share premium account in any way.

Purchase of Own Shares

35   Subject to the provisions of the Act, the company may purchase its own shares (including any redeemable shares) and, if it is a private company, make a payment in respect of the redemption or purchase of its own shares otherwise than out of distributable profits of the company or the proceeds of a fresh issue of shares.

General Meetings

36   All general meetings other than annual general meetings shall be called extraordinary general meetings.

37   The directors may call general meetings and, on the requisition of members pursuant to the provisions of the Act, shall forthwith proceed to convene an extraordinary general meeting for a date not later than eight weeks after receipt of the requisition. If there are not within the United Kingdom sufficient directors to call a general meeting, any director or any member of the company may call a general meeting.

Notice of General Meetings

38   An annual general meeting and an extraordinary general meeting called for the passing of a special resolution or a resolution appointing a person as a director shall be called by at least twenty-one clear days' notice. All other extraordinary general meetings shall be called by at least fourteen clear days' notice but a general meeting may be called by shorter notice if it is so agreed –

   (a) in the case of an annual general meeting, by all the members entitled to attend and vote thereat; and
   (b) in the case of any other meeting by a majority in number of the members having a right to attend and vote being a majority together holding not less than ninety-five per cent in nominal value of the shares giving that right.

The notice shall specify the time and place of the meeting and the general nature of the business to be transacted and, in the case of an annual general meeting, shall specify the meeting as such.

   Subject to the provisions of the articles and to any restrictions imposed on any shares, the notice shall be given to all the members, to all persons entitled to a share in consequence of the death or bankruptcy of a member and to the directors and auditors.

39   The accidental omission to give notice of a meeting to, or the non-receipt of notice of a meeting by, any person entitled to receive notice shall not invalidate the proceedings at that meeting.

Proceedings at General Meetings

40   No business shall be transacted at any meeting unless a quorum is present. Two persons entitled to vote upon the business to be transacted, each being a member or a proxy for a member or a duly authorised representative of a corporation, shall be a quorum.

41   If such a quorum is not present within half an hour from the time appointed for the meeting, or if during a meeting such a quorum ceases to be present, the meeting shall stand adjourned to the same day in the next week at the same time and place or to such time and place as the directors may determine.

42   The chairman, if any, of the board of directors or in his absence some other director nominated by the directors shall preside as chairman of the meeting, but if neither the chairman nor such other director (if any) be present within fifteen minutes after the time appointed for holding the meeting and willing to act, the directors present shall elect one of their number to be chairman and, if there is only one director present and willing to act, he shall be chairman.

43   If no director is willing to act as chairman, or if no director is present within fifteen minutes after the time appointed for holding the meeting, the members present and entitled to vote shall choose one of their number to be chairman.

44   A director shall, notwithstanding that he is not a member, be entitled to attend and speak at any general meeting and at any separate meeting of the holders of any class of shares in the company.

45   The chairman may, with the consent of a meeting at which a quorum is present (and shall if so directed by the meeting), adjourn the meeting from time to time and from place to place, but no business shall be transacted at an adjourned meeting other than business which might properly have been transacted at the meeting had the adjournment not taken place. When a meeting is adjourned for fourteen days or more, at least seven clear days' notice shall be given specifying the time and place of the adjourned meeting and the general nature of the business to be transacted. Otherwise it shall not be necessary to give any such notice.

46   A resolution put to the vote of a meeting shall be decided on a show of hands unless before, or on the declaration of the result of, the show of hands a poll is duly demanded. Subject to the provisions of the Act, a poll may be demanded:

  (a) by the chairman; or
  (b) by at least two members having the right to vote at the meeting; or
  (c) by a member or members representing not less than one-tenth of the total voting rights of all the members having the right to vote at the meeting; or
  (d) by a member or members holding shares conferring a right to vote at the meeting being shares on which an aggregate sum has been paid up equal to not less than one-tenth of the total sum paid up on all the shares conferring that right;

and a demand by a person as proxy for a member shall be the same as a demand by the member.

47   Unless a poll is duly demanded a declaration by the chairman that a resolution has been carried or carried unanimously, or by a particular majority, or lost, or not carried by a particular majority and an entry to that effect in the minutes of the meeting shall be conclusive evidence of the fact without proof of the number or proportion of the votes recorded in favour of or against the resolution.

48   The demand for a poll may, before the poll is taken, be withdrawn but only with the consent of the chairman and a demand so withdrawn shall not be taken to have invalidated the result of a show of hands declared before the demand was made.

49   A poll shall be taken as the chairman directs and he may appoint scrutineers (who need not be members) and fix a time and place for declaring the result of the poll. The result of the poll shall be deemed to be the resolution of the meeting at which the poll was demanded.

50   In the case of an equality of votes, whether on a show of hands or on a poll, the chairman shall be entitled to a casting vote in addition to any other vote he may have.

51   A poll demanded on the election of a chairman or on a question of adjournment shall be taken forthwith. A poll demanded on any other question shall be taken either forthwith or at such time and place as the chairman directs not being more than thirty days after the poll is demanded. The demand for a poll shall not prevent the continuance of a meeting for the transaction of any business other than the question on which the poll was demanded. If a poll is demanded before the declaration of the result of a show of hands and the demand is duly withdrawn, the meeting shall continue as if the demand had not been made.

52   No notice need be given of a poll not taken forthwith if the time and place at which it is to be taken are announced at the meeting at which it is demanded. In any other case at least seven clear days' notice shall be given specifying the time and place at which the poll is to be taken.

53   A resolution in writing executed by or on behalf of each member who would have been entitled to vote upon it if it had been proposed at a general meeting at which he was present shall be as effectual as if it had been passed as a general meeting duly convened and held and may consist of several instruments in the like form each executed by or on behalf of one or more members.

Votes of Members

54   Subject to any rights or restrictions attached to any shares, on a show of hands every member who (being an individual) is present in person or (being a corporation) is present by a duly authorised representative, not being himself a member entitled to vote, shall have one vote and on a poll every member shall have one vote for every share of which he is the holder.

55   In the case of joint holders the vote of the senior who tenders a vote, whether in person or by proxy, shall be accepted to the exclusion of the votes of the other joint holders; and seniority shall be determined by the order in which the names of the holders stand in the register of members.

56   A member in respect of whom an order has been made by any court having jurisdiction (whether in the United Kingdom or elsewhere) in matters concerning mental disorder may vote, whether on a show of hands or on a poll, by his receiver, curator bonis or other person authorised in that behalf appointed by that court, and any such receiver, curator bonis or other person may, on a poll, vote by proxy. Evidence to the satisfaction of the directors of the authority of the person claiming to exercise the right to vote shall be deposited at the office, or at such other place as is specified in accordance with the articles for the deposit of instruments of proxy, not less than 48 hours before the time appointed for holding the meeting or

adjourned meeting at which the right to vote is to be exercised and in default the right to vote shall not be exercisable.

57   No member shall vote at any general meeting or at any separate meeting of the holders of any class of shares in the company, either in person or by proxy, in respect of any share held by him unless all moneys presently payable by him in respect of that share have been paid.

58   No objection shall be raised to the qualification of any voter except at the meeting or adjourned meeting at which the vote objected to is tendered, and every vote not disallowed at the meeting shall be valid. Any objection made in due time shall be referred to the chairman whose decision shall be final and conclusive.

59   On a poll votes may be given either personally or by proxy. A member may appoint more than one proxy to attend on the same occasion.

60   The appointment of a proxy shall be ... executed by or on behalf of the appointor and shall be in the following form (or in a form as near thereto as circumstances allow or in any other form which is usual or which the directors may approve) –

'   PLC/Limited

I/We   , of   , being
a member/members of the above-named company, hereby appoint
of   , or failing him,
of   , as my/our proxy to vote in my/our names[s]
and on my/our behalf at the annual/extraordinary general meeting of the company
to be held on   20   , and at any adjournment thereof.
Signed on   20   .'

61   Where it is desired to afford members an opportunity of instructing the proxy how he shall act the appointment of a proxy shall be in the following form (or in a form as near thereto as circumstances allow or in any other form which is usual or which the directors may approve) –

'   PLC/Limited

I/We   , of   , being
a member/members of the above-named company, hereby appoint
of   , or failing him   ,
of   , as my/our proxy to vote in my/our name[s]
and on my/our behalf at the annual/extraordinary general meeting of the company, to be held on   20   , and at any adjournment thereof.
This form is to be used in respect of the resolutions mentioned below as follows:
      Resolution No.1 *for *against
      Resolution No.2 *for *against.
*Strike out whichever is not desired.
Unless otherwise instructed, the proxy may vote as he thinks fit or abstain from voting.
Signed this   day of   20   .'

62   The appointment of a proxy and any authority under which it is executed or a copy of such authority certified notarially or in some other way approved by the directors may –

(a) in the case of an instrument in writing be deposited at the office or at such other place within the United Kingdom as is specified in the notice convening the meeting or in any instrument of proxy sent out by the company in relation to the meeting not less than 48 hours before the time for holding the meeting or adjourned meeting at which the person named in the instrument proposes to vote; or

(aa) in the case of an appointment contained in an electronic communication, where an address has been specified for the purpose of receiving electronic communications –

    (i)   in the notice convening the meeting, or

    (ii) in any instrument of proxy sent out by the company in relation to the meeting, or

    (iii) in any invitation contained in an electronic communication to appoint a proxy issued by the company in relation to the meeting,

be received at such address not less than 48 hours before the time for holding the meeting or adjourned meeting at which the person named in the appointment proposes to vote;

(b) in the case of a poll taken more than 48 hours after it is demanded, be deposited or received as aforesaid after the poll has been demanded and not less than 24 hours before the time appointed for the taking of the poll; or

(c) where the poll is not taken forthwith but is taken not more than 48 hours after it was demanded, be delivered at the meeting at which the poll was demanded to the chairman or to the secretary or to any director;

and an appointment of proxy which is not deposited, delivered or received in a manner so permitted shall be invalid. In this regulation and the next, 'address', in relation to electronic communications, includes any number or address used for the purposes of such communications.

63   A vote given or poll demanded by proxy or by the duly authorised representative of a corporation shall be valid notwithstanding the previous determination of the authority of the person voting or demanding a poll unless notice of the determination was received by the company at the office or at such other place at which the instrument of proxy was duly deposited or, where the appointment of the proxy was contained in an electronic communication, at the address at which such appointment was duly received before the commencement of the meeting or adjourned meeting at which the vote is given or the poll demanded or (in the case of a poll taken otherwise than on the same day as the meeting or adjourned meeting) the time appointed for taking the poll.

Number of Directors

64   Unless otherwise determined by ordinary resolution, the number of directors (other than alternate directors) shall not be subject to any maximum but shall be not less than two.

Alternate Directors

65   Any director (other than an alternate director) may appoint any other director, or any other person approved by resolution of the directors and willing to act, to be an alternate director and may remove from office an alternate director so appointed by him.

66   An alternate director shall be entitled to receive notice of all meetings of directors and of all meetings of committees of directors of which his appointor is a member, to attend and vote at any such meeting at which the director appointing him is not personally present, and generally to perform all the functions of his appointor as a director in his absence but shall not be entitled to receive any remuneration from the company for his services as an alternate director. But it shall not be necessary to give notice of such a meeting to an alternate director who is absent from the United Kingdom.

67   An alternate director shall cease to be an alternate director if his appointor ceases to be a director; but, if a director retires by rotation or otherwise but is reappointed or deemed to have been reappointed at the meeting at which he retires, any appointment of an alternate director made by him which was in force immediately prior to his retirement shall continue after his reappointment.

68   Any appointment or removal of an alternate director shall be by notice to the company signed by the director making or revoking the appointment or in any other manner approved by the directors.

69   Save as otherwise provided in the articles, an alternate director shall be deemed for all purposes to be a director and shall alone be responsible for his own acts and defaults and he shall not be deemed to be the agent of the director appointing him.

Powers of Directors

70   Subject to the provisions of the Act, the memorandum and the articles and to any directions given by special resolution, the business of the company shall be managed by the directors who may exercise all the powers of the company. No alteration of the memorandum or articles and no such direction shall invalidate any prior act of the directors which would have been valid if that alteration had not been made or that direction had not been given. The powers given by this regulation shall not be limited by any special power given to the directors by the articles and a meeting of directors at which a quorum is present may exercise all powers exercisable by the directors.

71   The directors may, by power of attorney or otherwise, appoint any person to be the agent of the company for such purposes and on such conditions as they determine, including authority for the agent to delegate all or any of his powers.

Delegation of Directors' Powers

72   The directors may delegate any of their powers to any committee consisting of one or more directors. They may also delegate to any managing director or any director holding any other executive office such of their powers as they consider desirable to be exercised by him. Any such delegation may be made subject to any conditions the directors may impose, and either collaterally with or to the exclusion of their own powers and may be revoked or altered. Subject to any such conditions, the proceedings of a committee with two or more members shall be governed by the articles regulating the proceedings of directors so far as they are capable of applying.

Appointment and Retirement of Directors

73   At the first annual general meeting all the directors shall retire from office, and at every subsequent annual general meeting one-third of the directors who are subject to retirement by rotation or, if their number is not three or a multiple of

three, the number nearest to one-third shall retire from office; but, if there is only one director who is subject to retirement by rotation, he shall retire.

74   Subject to the provisions of the Act, the directors to retire by rotation shall be those who have been longest in office since their last appointment or reappointment, but as between persons who became or were last reappointed directors on the same day those to retire shall (unless they otherwise agree among themselves) be determined by lot.

75   If the company, at the meeting at which a director retires by rotation, does not fill the vacancy the retiring director shall, if willing to act, be deemed to have been reappointed unless at the meeting it is resolved not to fill the vacancy or unless a resolution for the reappointment of the directors is put to the meeting and lost.

76   No person other than a director retiring by rotation shall be appointed or reappointed a director at any general meeting unless:

(a) he is recommended by the directors; or
(b) not less than fourteen nor more than thirty-five clear days before the date appointed for the meeting, notice executed by a member qualified to vote at the meeting has been given to the company of the intention to propose that person for appointment or reappointment stating the particulars which would, if he were so appointed or reappointed, be required to be included in the company's register of directors together with notice executed by that person of his willingness to be appointed or reappointed.

77   Not less than seven nor more than twenty-eight clear days before the date appointed for holding a general meeting notice shall be given to all who are entitled to receive notice of the meeting of any person (other than a director retiring by rotation at the meeting) who is recommended by the directors for appointment or reappointment as a director at the meeting or in respect of whom notice has been duly given to the company of the intention to propose him at the meeting for appointment or reappointment as a director. The notice shall give the particulars of that person which would, if he were so appointed or reappointed, be required to be included in the company's register of directors.

78   Subject as aforesaid, the company may by ordinary resolution appoint a person who is willing to act to be a director either to fill a vacancy or as an additional director and may also determine the rotation in which any additional directors are to retire.

79   The directors may appoint a person who is willing to act to be a director, either to fill a vacancy or as an additional director, provided that the appointment does not cause the number of directors to exceed any number fixed by or in accordance with the articles as the maximum number of directors. A director so appointed shall hold office only until the next following annual general meeting and shall not be taken into account in determining the directors who are to retire by rotation at the meeting. If not reappointed at such annual general meeting, he shall vacate office at the conclusion thereof.

80   Subject as aforesaid, a director who retires at an annual general meeting may, if willing to act, be reappointed. If he is not reappointed, he shall retain office until the meeting appoints someone in his place, or if it does not do so, until the end of the meeting.

Disqualification and Removal of Directors

81   The office of a director shall be vacated if –

(a) he ceases to be a director by virtue of any provision of the Act or he becomes prohibited by law from being a director; or

(b) he becomes bankrupt or makes any arrangement or composition with his creditors generally; or

(c) he is, or may be, suffering from mental disorder and either:

    (i)   he is admitted to hospital in pursuance of an application for admission for treatment under the Mental Health Act 1983 or, in Scotland, an application for admission under the Mental Health (Scotland) Act 1960, or

    (ii) an order is made by a court having jurisdiction (whether in the United Kingdom or elsewhere) in matters concerning mental disorder for his detention or for the appointment of a receiver, curator bonis or other person to exercise powers with respect to his property or affairs; or

(d) he resigns his office by notice to the company; or

(e) he shall for more than six consecutive months have been absent without permission of the directors from meetings of directors held during that period and the directors resolve that his office be vacated.

Remuneration of Directors

82   The directors shall be entitled to such remuneration as the company may by ordinary resolution determine and, unless the resolution provides otherwise, the remuneration shall be deemed to accrue from day to day.

Directors' Expenses

83   The directors may be paid all travelling, hotel and other expenses properly incurred by them in connection with their attendance at meetings of directors or committees of directors or general meetings or separate meetings of the holders of any class of shares or of debentures of the company or otherwise in connection with the discharge of their duties.

Directors' Appointments and Interests

84   Subject to the provisions of the Act, the directors may appoint one or more of their number to the office of managing director or to any other executive office under the company and may enter into an agreement or arrangement with any director for his employment by the company or for the provision by him of any services outside the scope of the ordinary duties of a director. Any such appointment, agreement or arrangement may be made upon such terms as the directors determine and they may remunerate any such director for his services as they think fit. Any appointment of a director to an executive office shall terminate if he ceases to be a director but without prejudice to any claim to damages for breach of the contract of service between the director and the company. A managing director and a director holding any other executive office shall not be subject to retirement by rotation.

85   Subject to the provisions of the Act, and provided that he has disclosed to the

directors the nature and extent of any material interests of his, a director notwithstanding his office –

> (a) may be a party to, or otherwise interested in, any transaction or arrangement with the company or in which the company is otherwise interested;
> (b) may be a director or other officer of, or employed by, or a party to any transaction or arrangement with, or otherwise interested in, any body corporate promoted by the company or in which the company is otherwise interested; and
> (c) shall not, by reason of his office, be accountable to the company for any benefit which he derives from any such office or employment or from any such transaction or arrangement or from any interest in any such body corporate and no such transaction or arrangement shall be liable to be avoided on the ground of any such interest or benefit.

86   For the purposes of regulation 85 –

> (a) a general notice given to the directors that a director is to be regarded as having an interest of the nature and extent specified in the notice in any transaction or arrangement in which a specified person or class of persons is interested shall be deemed to be a disclosure that the director has an interest in any such transaction of the nature and extent so specified; and
> (b) an interest of which a director has no knowledge and of which it is unreasonable to expect him to have knowledge shall not be treated as an interest of his.

Directors' Gratuities and Pensions

87   The directors may provide benefits, whether by the payment of gratuities or pensions or by insurance or otherwise, for any director who has held but no longer holds any executive office or employment with the company or with any body corporate which is or has been a subsidiary of the company or a predecessor in business of the company or of any such subsidiary, and for any member of his family (including a spouse and a former spouse) or any person who is or was dependent on him, and may (as well before as after he ceases to hold such office or employment) contribute to any fund and pay premiums for the purchase or provision of any such benefit.

Proceedings of Directors

88   Subject to the provisions of the articles, the directors may regulate their proceedings as they think fit. A director may, and the secretary at the request of a director shall, call a meeting of the directors. It shall not be necessary to give notice of a meeting to a director who is absent from the United Kingdom. Questions arising at a meeting shall be decided by a majority of votes. In the case of an equality of votes, the chairman shall have a second or casting vote. A director who is also an alternate director shall be entitled in the absence of his appointor to a separate vote on behalf of his appointor in addition to his own vote.

89   The quorum for the transaction of the business of the directors may be fixed by the directors and unless so fixed at any other number shall be two. A person who holds office only as an alternate director shall, if his appointor is not present, be counted in the quorum.

90 The continuing directors or a sole continuing director may act notwithstanding any vacancies in their number, but, if the number of directors is less than the number fixed as the quorum, the continuing directors or director may act only for the purpose of filling vacancies or of calling a general meeting.

91 The directors may appoint one of their number to be the chairman of the board of directors and may at any time remove him from that office. Unless he is unwilling to do so, the director so appointed shall preside at every meeting of directors at which he is present. But if there is no director holding that office, or if the director holding it is unwilling to preside or is not present within five minutes after the time appointed for the meeting, the directors present may appoint one of their number to be chairman of the meeting.

92 All acts done by a meeting of directors, or of a committee of directors, or by a person acting as as director shall, notwithstanding that it be afterwards discovered that there was a defect in the appointment of any director or that any of them were disqualified from holding office, or had vacated office, or were not entitled to vote, be as valid as if every such person had been duly appointed and was qualified and had continued to be a director and had been entitled to vote.

93 A resolution in writing signed by all the directors entitled to receive notice of a meeting of directors or of a committee of directors shall be as valid and effectual as if it had been passed at a meeting of directors or (as the case may be) a committee of directors duly convened and held and may consist of several documents in the like form each signed by one or more directors; but a resolution signed by an alternate director need not also be signed by his appointor and, if it is signed by a director who has appointed an alternate director, it need not be signed by the alternate director in that capacity.

94 Save as otherwise provided by the articles, a director shall not vote at a meeting of directors or of a committee of directors on any resolution concerning a matter in which he has, directly or indirectly, an interest or duty which is material and which conflicts or may conflict with the interests of the company unless his interest or duty arises only because the case falls within one or more of the following paragraphs –

(a) the resolution relates to the giving to him of a guarantee, security, or indemnity in respect of money lent to, or an obligation incurred by him for the benefit of, the company or any of its subsidiaries;
(b) the resolution relates to the giving to a third party of a guarantee, security, or indemnity in respect of an obligation of the company or any of its subsidiaries for which the director has assumed responsibility in whole or part and whether alone or jointly with others under a guarantee or indemnity or by the giving of security;
(c) his interest arises by virtue of his subscribing or agreeing to subscribe for any shares, debentures or other securities of the company or any of its subsidiaries, or by virtue of his being, or intending to become, a participant in the underwriting or sub-underwriting of an offer of any such shares, debentures, or other securities by the company or any of its subsidiaries for subscription, purchase or exchange;
(d) the resolution relates in any way to a retirement benefits scheme which has been approved, or is conditional upon approval, by the Board of Inland Revenue for taxation purposes.

For the purposes of this regulation, an interest of a person who is, for any purpose of the Act (excluding any statutory modification thereof not in force when this regulation becomes binding on the company), connected with a director shall be treated as an interest of the director and, in relation to an alternate director without prejudice to any interest which the alternate director has otherwise.

95   A director shall not be counted in the quorum present at a meeting in relation to a resolution on which he is not entitled to vote.

96   The company may by ordinary resolution suspend or relax to any extent, either generally or in respect of any particular matter, any provision of the articles prohibiting a director from voting at a meeting of directors or of a committee of directors.

97   Where proposals are under consideration concerning the appointment of two or more directors to offices or employments with the company or any body corporate in which the company is interested the proposals may be divided and considered in relation to each director separately and (provided he is not for another reason precluded from voting) each of the directors concerned shall be entitled to vote and be counted in the quorum in respect of each resolution except that concerning his own appointment.

98   If a question arises at a meeting of directors or of a committee of directors as to the right of a director to vote, the question may, before the conclusion of the meeting, be referred to the chairman of the meeting and his ruling in relation to any director other than himself shall be final and conclusive.

Secretary

99   Subject to the provisions of the Act, the secretary shall be appointed by the directors for such term, at such remuneration and upon such conditions as they may think fit; and any secretary so appointed may be removed by them.

Minutes

100   The directors shall cause minutes to be made in books kept for the purpose –

   (a) of all appointments of officers made by the directors; and
   (b) of all proceedings at the meetings of the company, of the holders of any class of shares in the company, and of the directors, and of committees of directors, including the names of the directors present at each such meeting.

The Seal

101   The seal shall only be used by the authority of the directors or of a committee of directors authorised by the directors. The directors may determine who shall sign any instrument to which the seal is affixed and unless otherwise so determined it shall be signed by a director and by the secretary or by a second director.

Dividends

102   Subject to the provisions of the Act, the company may by ordinary resolution declare dividends in accordance with the respective rights of the members, but no dividend shall exceed the amount recommended by the directors.

103   Subject to the provisions of the Act, the directors may pay interim dividends if it appears to them that they are justified by the profits of the company available for

distribution. If the share capital is divided into different classes, the directors may pay interim dividends on shares which confer deferred or non-preferred rights with regard to dividend as well as on shares which confer preferential rights with regard to dividend, but no interim dividend shall be paid on shares carrying deferred or non-preferred rights if, at the time of payment, any preferential dividend is in arrears. The directors may also pay at intervals settled by them any dividend payable at a fixed rate if it appears to them that the profits available for distribution justify the payment. Provided the directors act in good faith they shall not incur any liability to the holders of shares conferring preferred rights for any loss they may suffer by the lawful payment of an interim dividend on any shares having deferred or non-preferred rights.

104 Except as otherwise provided by the rights attached to shares, all dividends shall be declared and paid according to the amounts paid up on the shares on which the dividend is paid. All dividends shall be apportioned and paid proportionately to the amounts paid up on the shares during any portion or portions of the period in respect of which the dividend is paid; but, if any share is issued on terms providing that it shall rank for dividend as from a particular date, that share shall rank for dividend accordingly.

105 A general meeting declaring a dividend may, upon the recommendation of the directors, direct that it shall be satisfied wholly or partly by the distribution of assets and, where any difficulty arises in regard to the distribution, the directors may settle the same and in particular may issue fractional certificates and fix the value for distribution of any assets and may determine that cash shall be paid to any member upon the footing of the value so fixed in order to adjust the rights of members and may vest any assets in trustees.

106 Any dividend or other moneys payable in respect of a share may be paid by cheque sent by post to the registered address of the person entitled or, if two or more persons are the holders of the share or are jointly entitled to it by reason of the death or bankruptcy of the holder, to the registered address of that one of those persons who is first named in the register of members or to such person and to such address as the person or persons entitled may in writing direct. Every cheque shall be made payable to the order of the person or persons entitled or to such other person as the person or persons entitled may in writing direct and payment of the cheque shall be a good discharge to the company. Any joint holder or other person jointly entitled to a share as aforesaid may give receipts for any dividend or other moneys payable in respect of the share.

107 No dividend or other moneys payable in respect of a share shall bear interest against the company unless otherwise provided by the rights attached to the share.

108 Any dividend which has remained unclaimed for twelve years from the date when it became due for payment shall, if the directors so resolve, be forfeited and cease to remain owing by the company.

Accounts

109 No member shall (as such) have any right of inspecting any accounting records or other book or document of the company except as conferred by statute or authorised by the directors or by ordinary resolution of the company.

Capitalisation of Profits

110 The directors may with the authority of an ordinary resolution of the company –

(a) subject as hereinafter provided, resolve to capitalise any undivided profits of the company not required for paying any preferential dividend (whether or not they are available for distribution) or any sum standing to the credit of the company's share premium account or capital redemption reserve;

(b) appropriate the sum resolved to be capitalised to the members who would have been entitled to it if it were distributed by way of dividend and in the same proportions and apply such sum on their behalf either in or towards paying up the amounts, if any, for the time being unpaid on any shares held by them respectively, or in paying up in full unissued shares or debentures of the company of a nominal amount equal to that sum, and allot the shares or debentures credited as fully paid to those members, or as they may direct, in those proportions, or partly in one way and partly in the other: but the share premium account, the capital redemption reserve, and any profits which are not available for distribution may, for the purposes of this regulation, only be applied in paying up unissued shares to be allotted to members credited as fully paid;

(c) make such provision by the issue of fractional certificates or by payment in cash or otherwise as they determine in the case of shares or debentures becoming distributable under this regulation in fractions; and

(d) authorise any person to enter on behalf of all the members concerned into an agreement with the company providing for the allotment to them respectively, credited as fully paid, of any shares or debentures to which they are entitled upon such capitalisation, any agreement made under such authority being binding on all such members.

Notices

111   Any notice to be given to or by any person pursuant to the articles (other than a notice calling a meeting of the directors) shall be in writing or shall be given using electronic communications to an address for the time being notified for that purpose to the person giving the notice.

In this regulation, 'address', in relation to electronic communications, includes any number or address used for the purposes of such communications.

112   The company may give any notice to a member either personally or by sending it by post in a prepaid envelope addressed to the member at his registered address or by leaving it at that address or by giving it using electronic communications to an address for the time being notified to the company by the member. In the case of joint holders of a share, all notices shall be given to the joint holder whose name stands first in the register of members in respect of the joint holding and notice so given shall be sufficient notice to all the joint holders. A member whose registered address is not within the United Kingdom and who gives to the company an address within the United Kingdom at which notices may be given to him, or an address to which notices may be sent using electronic communications, shall be entitled to have notices given to him at that address, but otherwise no such member shall be entitled to receive any notice from the company.

In this regulation and the next, 'address', in relation to electronic communications, includes any number or address used for the purposes of such communications.

113   A member present, either in person or by proxy, at any meeting of the company or of the holders of any class of shares in the company shall be deemed to

have received notice of the meeting and, where requisite, of the purposes for which it was called.

114 Every person who becomes entitled to a share shall be bound by any notice in respect of that share which, before his name is entered in the register of members, has been duly given to a person from whom he derives his title.

115 Proof that an envelope containing a notice was properly addressed, prepaid and posted shall be conclusive evidence that the notice was given. Proof that a notice contained in an electronic communication was sent in accordance with guidance issued by the Institute of Chartered Secretaries and Administrators shall be conclusive evidence that the notice was given. A notice shall, be deemed to be given at the expiration of 48 hours after the envelope containing it was posted or, in the case of a notice contained in an electronic communication, at the expiration of 48 hours after the time it was sent.

116 A notice may be given by the company to the persons entitled to a share in consequence of the death or bankruptcy of a member by sending or delivering it, in any manner authorised by the articles for the giving of notice to a member, addressed to them by name, or by the title of representatives of the deceased, or trustee of the bankrupt or by any like description at the address, if any, within the United Kingdom supplied for that purpose by the persons claiming to be so entitled. Until such an address has been supplied, a notice may be given in any manner in which it might have been given if the death or bankruptcy had not occurred.

Winding Up

117 If the company is wound up, the liquidator may, with the sanction of an extraordinary resolution of the company and any other sanction required by the Act, divide among the members in specie the whole or any part of the assets of the company and may, for that purpose, value any assets and determine how the division shall be carried out as between the members or different classes of members. The liquidator may, with the like sanction, vest the whole or any part of the assets in trustees upon such trusts for the benefit of the members as he with the like sanction determines, but no member shall be compelled to accept any assets upon which there is a liability.

Indemnity

118 Subject to the provisions of the Act but without prejudice to any indemnity to which a director may otherwise be entitled, every director or other officer or auditor of the company shall be indemnified out of the assets of the company against any liability incurred by him in defending any proceedings, whether civil or criminal, in which judgment is given in his favour or in which he is acquitted or in connection with an application in which relief is granted to him by the court from liability for negligence, default, breach of duty or breach of trust in relation to the affairs of the company.

Index